Basic Edition
# English for Everyday Activities
## A Picture Process Dictionary

*Lawrence J. Zwier*
*Adapted by Janet Podnecky*
*Course Crafters, Inc.*

Paul     Kate     Alex     Tom     Jenny     Pam     Dan

**New Readers Press**

English for Everyday Activities: A Picture Process Dictionary Basic Edition
ISBN 978-1-56420-284-0
Copyright © 1999
Asia-Pacific Press Holdings Ltd, Hong Kong
Adapted by New Readers Press 2002
New material for this adapted edition Copyright © 2002 New Readers Press
A Publishing Division of ProLiteracy
1320 Jamesville Avenue, Syracuse, New York 13210

This adapted edition is for sale in the USA and Canada only.

Printed in the United States of America
9  8  7  6

**Acquisitions Editor:** Paula L. Schlusberg
**Production Director:** Heather Witt
**Cover Designer:** Kimbrly Koennecke

Student Book Design and Illustration by Yohan Publications, Inc. Tokyo
**Illustrations:** Nozumi Kudo
**Design:** Makiko Ito/SPACE U

Development and production of this adapted edition by
Course Crafters, Inc., Newburyport, MA

All proceeds from the sale of New Readers Press materials support literacy
programs in the United States and worldwide.

# Table of Contents

To the Student                                                                      5

---

**SECTION 1: STARTING THE DAY**

1   First Thing in the Morning                                               6–7
2   Brushing Your Teeth / Flossing                                             8
3   Taking a Shower                                                            9
4   Getting Dressed — A Man                                               10–11
5   Getting Dressed — A Woman                                            12–13
6   Making a Bed                                                              14
    Making Breakfast
7   Making Coffee / Making Tea                                               15
8   Preparing Cold Cereal / Making Toast                                     16
9   Frying an Egg                                                            17
10  Eating Breakfast                                                         18
11  Leaving the House                                                        19

---

**SECTION 2: GETTING AROUND**

12  Taking a Bus                                                         20–21
    Driving a Car
13  Starting Out                                                             22
14  Driving                                                                  23
15  Driving Along                                                        24–25
16  Taking a Train                                                           26
17  Taking a Taxi                                                            27
18  Walking Somewhere                                                        28
19  Riding a Bicycle                                                         29

---

**SECTION 3: AT HOME IN THE EVENING**

20  Returning Home                                                       30–31
    Making Dinner
21  Making a Salad                                                           32
22  Preparing Vegetables                                                     33
23  Making Spaghetti                                                     34–35
24  Cooking Rice                                                             36
25  Eating Dinner                                                            37
26  Clearing the Table                                                       38
27  Doing Dishes                                                             39
    Relaxing at Home
28  Playing a CD (Compact Disc)                                             40
29  Using a Cassette Player                                                 41
30  Reading                                                                  42
31  Watching Television                                                      43

| 32 | Watching a Video | 44 |
| 33 | Babysitting | 45 |
| 34 | Going to Bed | 46–47 |

## SECTION 4: MANAGING A HOUSEHOLD

| 35 | Doing Laundry | 48–49 |
| 36 | Cleaning the House | 50–51 |
|  | Taking Care of Pets | |
| 37 | Taking Care of a Cat | 52 |
| 38 | Taking Care of a Dog | 53 |
| 39 | Taking Care of a Lawn | 54 |
| 40 | Gardening | 55 |
| 41 | Cleaning a Car | 56 |
| 42 | Taking a Car to the Garage for Repairs | 57 |
| 43 | Changing a Flat Tire | 58 |
| 44 | Dealing with a Power Failure | 59 |
| 45 | Working with Wood | 60 |
| 46 | Joining Things with Bolts / Screws | 61 |
| 47 | Shopping for Groceries | 62–63 |
| 48 | Paying for Things | 64–65 |
| 49 | Going to a Bank | 66 |
| 50 | Using an ATM | 67 |

## SECTION 5: KEEPING IN TOUCH

|  | Using the Telephone | |
| 51 | Making a Phone Call | 68 |
| 52 | Answering a Telephone | 69 |
| 53 | Leaving a Message | 70 |
| 54 | Taking a Message | 71 |
| 55 | Using an Answering Machine | 72 |
| 56 | Writing a Personal Letter | 73 |
| 57 | Mailing a Letter | 74–75 |

## SECTION 6: HAVING FUN WITH FRIENDS

| 58 | Going to a Birthday Party | 76 |
| 59 | Going to a Dinner Party | 77 |
| 60 | Going to a Movie | 78 |
| 61 | Eating at a Fast Food Restaurant | 79 |

| Common Measurements, Days, Months, and Numbers | 80–81 |
| Index | 82–88 |
| Irregular Forms | 89 |
| Processes — My Way | 90–95 |
| Notes to the Teacher | 96 |

# To the Student

Basic *English for Everyday Activities* teaches you vocabulary for talking about things you do every day. Here you will find English words for familiar objects and actions. In the pictures, you will see what the new vocabulary means. Listen to the recorded version of the book (available separately) to learn how the key vocabulary is spoken.

Basic *English for Everyday Activities* focuses on verbs—words for doing or acting. With these verbs, you can speak or write more clearly about your life. It also teaches nouns and other words that are used to talk about actions expressed by the verbs.

## Organization

Each chapter is about a process (how to do something). The chapters are grouped into six larger sections, and each one is about some aspect of everyday life. You may use the chapters in any order you like. For example, you can go from Chapter 10 ("Eating Breakfast") to Chapter 33 ("Babysitting") and then to Chapter 12 ("Taking a Bus") if you like.

Each chapter has a list of "key vocabulary"—the most important words and phrases from the chapter. The meanings of the key vocabulary are shown in the pictures. Each chapter also has a For Special Attention section to explain some key vocabulary.

At the back of the book is a section about U.S. measurements and money to help you understand the amounts mentioned in the text. You will also find charts of days of the week, months of the year, and numbers. Then there is a complete index of key vocabulary. Following this is a chart of the verbs *be* and *have* in the present tense and a list of some irregular noun forms used in the book.

## How to Use Basic *English for Everyday Activities*

You can use this book in a class or by yourself at home. If you are studying by yourself, think about what you do during the day—brush your teeth, take a bus, etc. How do you describe each process in English? Find the process in this book and study the pictures and words together. Use the pictures to help you remember the words. Think of the new words the next time you take part in one of the pictured actions. Use the workbook that goes with this book (available separately) to help you review and remember.

You can use the index to learn new vocabulary. If you learn a new word in one lesson, look it up in the index and notice the other pages where it appears. Turn to these pages to see the word in other contexts. For example, you may learn the word *rinse* as something you do in the shower; in the index, you will find that *rinse* is also used to talk about dishes, cars, and other things.

If you have an idea, but you don't know the words for it:
1. go to the table of contents,
2. look for an activity related to your idea,
3. go to the chapter and look at the pictures,
4. read the English related to the pictures.

If you can't find the right process in the table of contents, go through the pages until you see some pictures about your idea.

## Other Hints
- After you find a word you are interested in, read the whole chapter where you found it. Your word may be in the chapter more than once.
- Notice how the word fits into sentences. Learning a new vocabulary word means learning how it works with other words.
- Think about differences between how you do an activity and how it is described in the book. No two people's lives are exactly the same. Try using your new vocabulary to describe the activity your way, instead of the way it is in the book. This is an excellent way to make this new vocabulary your own.

# 1    First Thing in the Morning

## Key Vocabulary

**VERBS**
brush
dry off
eat
flush
get dressed
get up
go into
go out
make
shave
take (a shower)
use
wake up
wash

**NOUNS**
alarm clock
bathroom
breakfast
hair
hand
shower
toilet
tooth (teeth)
towel

## For Special Attention

- **wake up** — to stop sleeping
- **take a shower** — to wash yourself in a shower (You can also **take a bath.**)
- **use the toilet** — You can also say "use the bathroom" or "go to the bathroom."
- **flush the toilet** — to push the handle and make water clean the toilet

It's 7:00.

Dan wakes up.

He gets up.

He goes into the bathroom.

Dan uses the toilet.
Then he flushes it.

He washes his hands.

6

He brushes his teeth (see p. 8).

He shaves.

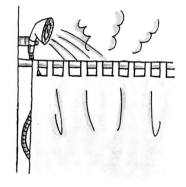
He takes a shower (see p. 9).

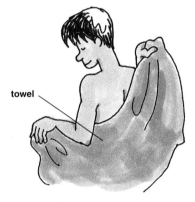
towel

He dries off.

Then he brushes his hair.

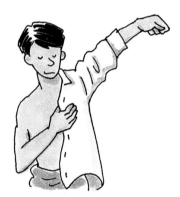
He gets dressed (see pp. 10–13).

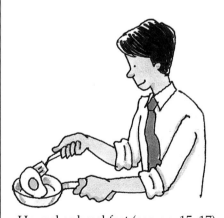
He makes breakfast (see pp. 15–17).

He eats it (see p. 18).

Then he goes out (see p. 19).

## Key Vocabulary

**VERBS**
brush
floss
move
pull out
put
put away
rinse (off)
run water over
slip
spit
swish
take

**NOUNS**
floss
mouth
sink
tooth (teeth)
toothbrush
toothpaste
water

**OTHERS**
back and forth (adverbial)
between (prep.)
up and down (adverbial)

## For Special Attention

- **back and forth** — something goes from one side to another (← and →) many times
- **up and down** — something goes in these directions (↑ and ↓) many times
- **slip** something — to carefully move something into a small place

Jenny runs water over her toothbrush.

She puts toothpaste on it.

She brushes up and down.

She brushes back and forth.

She rinses her mouth. She takes some water.

She swishes it back and forth.

Jenny spits the water into the sink.

She rinses off her toothbrush.

Then she puts it away.

### Jenny flosses her teeth.

She pulls out some floss.

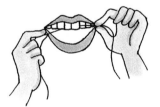

She slips it between her teeth.

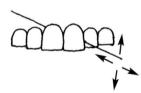

She moves it back and forth and up and down.

## Key Vocabulary

**VERBS**
close
dry
dry off
put
rinse off
step
take (a shower)
turn off
turn on
wash
wrap

**NOUNS**
arm
blow-dryer
curtain
deodorant
hair
shampoo
shower
soap
towel
water

## For Special Attention

- **dry off** — to dry the water on top of something (You "dry off" a table. You don't "dry off" your hair or a towel. You "dry" them.)
- **turn on** — to make something run or work
- **turn off** — to make something stop
- **deodorant** — something that takes away bad smells

Dan closes the shower curtain.

He turns on the water.

He washes his hair with shampoo.

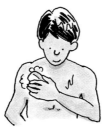

He washes himself with soap.

Then he rinses off with water.

He turns off the water.

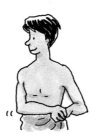

Dan steps out of the shower.

He takes a towel.

Then he dries himself off.

He wraps a towel around himself.

He dries his hair.

He puts deodorant under his arms.

## Key Vocabulary

**VERBS**
buckle
button
choose
fasten
get dressed
lace up
pick up
pull up
put on
slip on
snap
straighten
tie
tuck in
zip up

**NOUNS**
belt
buckle
button
collar
fastener
glasses
jacket
lace
man
pajamas
pants
shirt
shoe
shorts
snap
sock
T-shirt
underpants
underwear
zipper

**ADJECTIVE**
some

### Tom puts on...

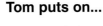

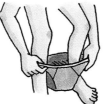   

...some underwear, | ...a T-shirt, | ...some socks, | ...pants,

...and a shirt.

Tom **puts on** his underwear.
Tom **puts** his underwear **on**.

These mean the same.

Tom chooses some socks and **puts them on**.

Tom picks up his shirt and **puts it on**.

With **it** or **them**, "on" moves away from "put."

### A? or Some?

 some pants

 some socks

 some shorts

 some underwear
some underpants

 a T-shirt

 some shoes

 a jacket

 some pajamas

 a shirt

 some glasses

You can say:
"a sock,"
"a shoe."

BUT

Do NOT say:
"a pant," "a pajama,"
"an underpant," "a short,"
"a glass."

10

## Putting on Pants

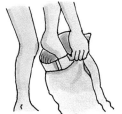
Tom puts on his pants.

He pulls them up.

He fastens them.

He zips up the pants.

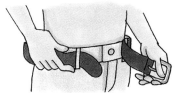
He slips on a belt.

He buckles it.

## Putting on a Shirt

Tom puts on his shirt.

He buttons it.

He straightens his collar.

He tucks in his shirt.

| Fasteners | What you do |
|---|---|
|  snap | You snap it. |
|  zipper | You zip it up. |
|  button | You button it. |
|  laces | You lace them up and then you tie the laces. |
|  buckle | You buckle it. |

## Key Vocabulary

**VERBS**
get dressed
go barefoot
put on
wear

**NOUNS**
blouse
boot
bra
cap
clothes
coat
dress
glove
hat
jacket
jeans
mitten
panties
pants
pantyhose
people
running shoe
sandal
scarf
shirt
shoe
shorts
skirt
sock
stocking
suit
sweater
sweatshirt
tie
T-shirt
weather
woman

**ADJECTIVES**
casual          light
cold            long-sleeved
heavy           short-sleeved
hot

Pam puts on…

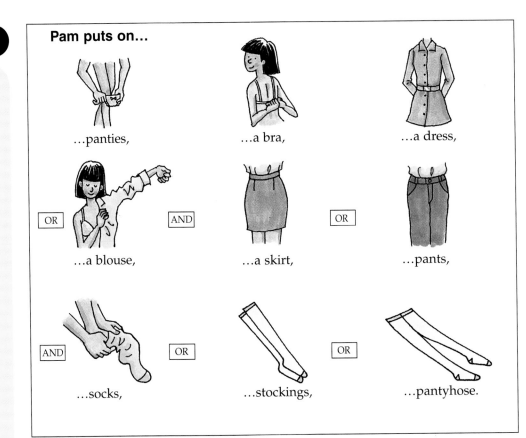

…panties,

…a bra,

…a dress,

OR …a blouse, AND …a skirt, OR …pants,

AND …socks, OR …stockings, OR …pantyhose.

## For Special Attention

- **go barefoot** — to walk around with no shoes or socks
- First you **put on** clothes. Then you **wear** them.
- To talk about the weather:
  1. Use *it* + *BE* + an adjective:
     - It is hot.
     - It is cold.
  2. Use *it* + *BE* + the *-ing* form of a weather verb:
     - It is raining.
     - It is snowing.

These people are wearing suits.

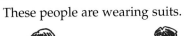
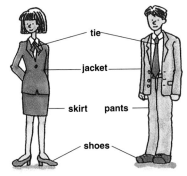

tie
jacket
skirt    pants
shoes

These people are wearing casual clothes.

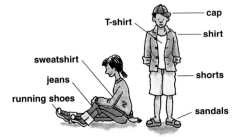

cap
T-shirt
shirt
sweatshirt
jeans
shorts
running shoes
sandals

12

## Dressing for Hot Weather

In hot weather, Pam wears light clothes:

…a short-sleeved shirt…

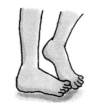

…and shorts.

She goes barefoot,

OR

…she wears sandals.

## Dressing for Cold Weather

In cold weather, Pam wears heavy clothes:

…a long-sleeved shirt,

…a sweater,

…pants,

…and heavy socks.

She puts on
a heavy coat…

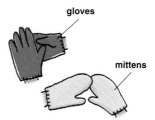

gloves

mittens

…and gloves
or mittens.

She puts on a scarf,

…a hat,

…and boots.

# Making a Bed

## Key Vocabulary

**VERBS**
fluff up
make a bed
pull
pull up
put
slip
smooth out
tuck

**NOUNS**
bed
bedspread
blanket
foot
head
mattress
pillow
sheet

**OTHERS**
bottom (adj.)
fitted (adj.)
flat (adj.)
over (prep.)
top (adj.)
under (prep.)

## For Special Attention

- You put your head near the **head of the bed** and your feet near the **foot of the bed.**
- A **pillow** goes inside a pillowcase.
- A **fitted sheet** has special corners to fit over the mattress. Fitted sheets are used only as bottom sheets, not as top sheets.
- **smooth out** a blanket — to make it straight and flat

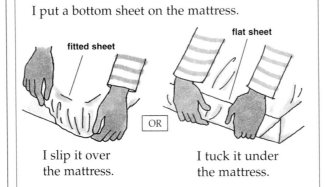

I put a bottom sheet on the mattress.

fitted sheet

flat sheet

OR

I slip it over the mattress.

I tuck it under the mattress.

Then I put on a top sheet. I tuck it under the foot of the bed.

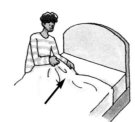

I pull up the top sheet.

I put a blanket on the bed.

I smooth it out.

I put a bedspread over the bed.

I fluff up the pillows.

I put them at the head of the bed.

I pull the bedspread over the pillows.

I smooth it out.

base form. when I don't a expesitica

to - run ⟶ en infinitivo
                    infinitive

Tom will put on a jacket
He will zip it up.
He will put on his houes
He will pick up his keys and wallet
Tom will put them in his pockets
He will picks up his backpack

Past              futered.
dipped.        will. dip.        diping.
stopped.       will stop.  stoping

go    will.go    went    gone

    Doble  consonants
        do bout
Brincar.   hopped.

# 7

# Making Coffee / Making Tea

## Key Vocabulary

**VERBS**
add
become
boil
drip
heat up
make
pour
put
stir
strain
turn on
wait

**NOUNS**
coffee
coffeemaker
coffeepot
filter
leaves
strainer
sugar
tea
teacup
teapot
water

**ADJECTIVES**
electric
ground
hot

## For Special Attention

• A **filter** has very small holes in it. Water or another liquid can pass through the holes, but the ground coffee cannot. A **strainer** does the same thing, but the holes are larger, and it has a handle.
• You grind coffee beans to make **ground coffee.**
• **heat up** — to become hot

### Making Coffee (with an electric coffeemaker)

Pam puts ground coffee into the filter.

Then she pours water into the coffeemaker.

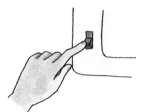

She turns on the coffeemaker.

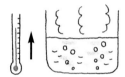

The water heats up.

It drips through the filter.

It drips into the coffeepot.

### Making Tea

Dan boils water.

He pours the hot water into a teapot.

He adds tea leaves.

Dan waits.

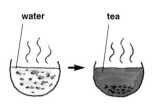

The water becomes tea.

Dan strains the tea.

Then he adds sugar and stirs the tea.

# 8 Preparing Cold Cereal / Making Toast

## Key Vocabulary

**VERBS**
make
peel
pop up
pour
prepare
push down
put on
slice
toast

**NOUNS**
banana
bowl
box
bread
butter
cereal
jam
knife
lever
milk
slice
sugar
toast
toaster

**ADJECTIVES**
cold
done

## For Special Attention

- **pop up** — to come up quickly
- **peel** fruit or vegetables — to take off the skin of the fruit or vegetable
- **slice** something — to cut it into thin pieces

### Preparing Cold Cereal

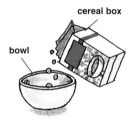
Pam pours cereal into a bowl.

She pours milk into the bowl.

She puts sugar on her cereal.

Then she peels a banana.

She slices it.

She puts the slices of banana on her cereal.

### Making Toast

Dan puts slices of bread into the toaster.

He pushes down the lever.

The toaster toasts the bread.

The toast is done. It pops up.

Dan puts butter and jam on his toast.

# 9

# Frying an Egg

## Key Vocabulary

**VERBS**
flip
fry
light
melt
put into
put on
take out
throw out
turn on

**NOUNS**
burner
butter
egg
frying pan
pan
plate
shell
stove
white
yolk

## For Special Attention

- **The egg fries.** — Dan fries the egg.
- Dan has a **gas** stove. Some people have electric stoves.
- **flip** something — to turn it upside down
- **throw out** — to put in the garbage
- **melt** something — to heat it until it changes to liquid

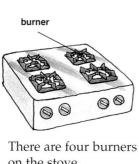
burner

There are four burners on the stove.

Dan turns on a burner.

It lights.

He puts a frying pan on the burner.

He melts butter in the pan.

He puts an egg into the pan.

Dan throws out the shell.

The egg fries.

He flips the egg.

plate

He takes it out of the pan.

He puts the egg on a plate.

**An egg:**

the white    the yolk

the shell

# 10 Eating Breakfast

## Key Vocabulary

**VERBS**
dip — *dipped.* *will dip.*
drink *dronk*
eat
finish
have (has)
leave
read
sit down
talk
wipe

**NOUNS**
bacon
bowl
breakfast
cereal
coffee
egg
fork
knife
mouth
napkin
paper
spoon
table
tea
toast

**OTHERS**
some (adj.)
sometimes (adv.)

## For Special Attention

- **the paper** — the newspaper
- First you **sit down.** Then you sit.
- You **dip** something into a liquid. You put it in for a short time. (See p. 35 for **"liquids and solids."**)

Pam and Dan sit down.

Pam drinks some coffee.

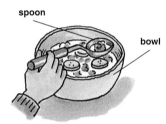

She eats some cereal.

Dan drinks some tea.

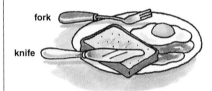

He has an egg with bacon and toast.

He dips his toast into the egg.

Sometimes they read the paper.

It says here that taxes are going up.

As usual...

Sometimes they talk.

Pam and Dan finish. They wipe their mouths with their napkins.

They leave the table.

## Key Vocabulary

**VERBS**
leave
open
pick up
put in
put on
say good-bye
shut
step
zip up

**NOUNS**
backpack
door
house
jacket
key
pocket
shoe
wallet

**ADVERB**
outside

## For Special Attention

- Some ways people **say good-bye:** "See you later."
  "Bye."
  "See you."
  "Good-bye."
- **leave the house** — You can also say "leave home."
- The opposite of **zip up** is "unzip."
- **shut the door** — to close the door

Tom puts on a jacket.

He zips it up.

He puts on his shoes.

He picks up his keys and wallet.

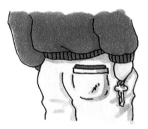

Tom puts them in his pockets.

He picks up his backpack.

Bye, Tom

See you later, Jenny.

Then Tom says good-bye to Jenny.

He opens the door.

He steps outside.

He shuts the door.

19

# 12 Taking a Bus

## Key Vocabulary

**VERBS**

| | |
|---|---|
| arrive | put |
| check | read |
| get off | show |
| get on | sit down |
| give | stand |
| hold on | stop |
| open | wait |
| pay | walk |
| press | |

**NOUNS**

| | |
|---|---|
| box | money |
| bus | pass |
| button | people |
| card | receipt |
| door | ride |
| driver | schedule |
| fare | seat |
| machine | stop |
| man | strap |

**OTHERS**

empty (adj.)
full (adj.)
near (prep.)
on time (adverbial)
other (adj.)
sometimes (adv.)

## For Special Attention

- **on time** — not late, not early
- **check a schedule** — look at a schedule to find information

- **bus pass** — a card or paper that is shown as payment for riding the bus (A bus pass is good for a few days, one week, or one month. When you have a bus pass, you don't pay on the bus.)

Jenny checks the bus schedule.

Bus 77 arrives at 8:20.

Jenny walks to the bus stop.

She sits down and waits.

The bus arrives on time.

The driver opens the door.

Jenny gets on the bus.

   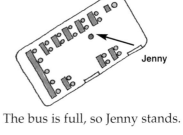

She shows her bus pass to the driver.

Other people pay their fare.

The bus is full, so Jenny stands.

strap

She holds on to a strap.

A man gets off the bus. A seat is empty.

Jenny sits down and reads.

Near her stop, she presses a button.

The driver stops the bus.

She gets off.

## Paying Bus Fare
People pay for a bus ride in many ways.

They put money into the fare box.

They pay the driver.

They put a fare card into a machine.

receipt

Sometimes, the driver or machine gives a receipt.

# 13 Starting Out

## Key Vocabulary

**VERBS**
back out of
buckle
fix
look
move
put in
sit
start
turn

**NOUNS**
car
driver
driveway
friend
key
mirror
seat
seat belt

**PREPOSITION**
behind

## For Special Attention

- You **fix** the mirror. — You move it until it is right.
- A **driveway** goes from the road to a building.

Kate's friends      Kate

Kate sits in the driver's seat.

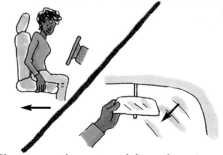

She moves the seat and fixes the mirror.

She buckles her seat belt.

Kate puts the key in.

She turns the key.

She starts the car.

Kate looks behind her.

driveway

Then she backs out of the driveway.

# 14 Driving

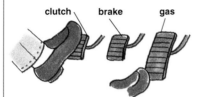

## Key Vocabulary

### VERBS
| | |
|---|---|
| go | speed up |
| let up on | step |
| put on | stop |
| rain | take off |
| shift | turn |
| slow down | turn on |

### NOUNS
| | |
|---|---|
| brake | light |
| car | neutral |
| clutch | night |
| foot | pedal |
| gas | signal |
| gear | steering wheel |
| gearshift | wiper |

### OTHERS
dark (adj.)
down (adv.)
fast (adv.)
sometimes (adv.)
up (adv.)

## For Special Attention

- **slow down** — to go slower
- **step on the gas** — to press the gas pedal
- **let up on the gas** — to put less pressure on the gas pedal
- **shift gears** — to change from one gear to another
- **shift up** — to change to a higher gear
- **shift down** — to change to a lower gear
- **Gears:**
  1 = first
  2 = second
  3 = third
  4 = fourth
  R = reverse
  Between gears is neutral.

## Shifting Gears

Pedals:

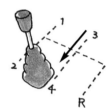

Kate steps on the clutch.

She shifts gears.

Then she takes her foot off the clutch.

## Speeding Up / Slowing Down

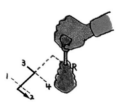

Kate steps on the gas.

The car goes faster.

She shifts up.

Kate lets up on the gas.

She shifts down.

The car slows down.

## Stopping

Kate steps on the brake.

## Turning

Kate puts her signal on.

She turns the steering wheel.

At night it gets dark.

Kate turns on the lights.

Sometimes it rains.

She turns on the wipers.

# 15 Driving Along

## Key Vocabulary

### VERBS
| | |
|---|---|
| change | park |
| check | pass |
| drive | pay |
| enter | pull over |
| exit | pump |
| get off | stop |
| get on | tell |
| get out | turn |
| give | turn off |
| go | want |
| go over | yield |
| lock | |

### NOUNS
| | |
|---|---|
| attendant | oil |
| car | police |
| driver | pump |
| freeway | right of way |
| friend | road |
| gas | side |
| gas station | sign |
| intersection | speed limit |
| lane | speeding |
| light | ticket |
| officer | traffic light |

### OTHERS
| | |
|---|---|
| ahead (adv.) | red (adj.) |
| green (adj.) | right (adv.) |
| left (adv.) | straight (adv.) |

## For Special Attention

- **turn green** — to become green
- **pull over** — to drive to the side of the road and stop
- **go over** a speed limit — to go too fast
- The attendant pumps the gas for Kate. Most people pump their own gas.

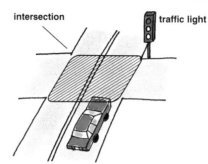

Kate stops for a red light.

The light turns green. Kate goes ahead.

She goes over the speed limit.

You were speeding, ma'am.

Really, Officer? Sorry.

A police officer gives her a ticket.

Kate parks the car.

She turns the car off.

Kate and her friends get out.

Kate locks the car.

## Some Things Drivers Do

Change lanes.

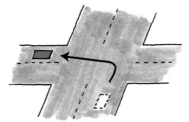
Turn left.

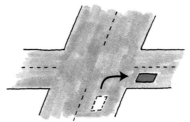
Turn right.

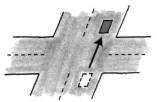
Go straight.

Get on (enter) a freeway.

Get off (exit) a freeway.

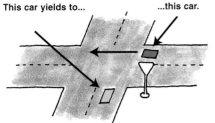
This car yields to... ...this car.
Yield right of way.

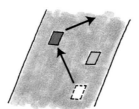
Pass someone.

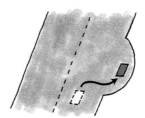
Pull over to the side of the road.

## Stopping for Gas

Kate goes to a gas station.

pump
She stops at a pump.

Yes, ma'am
Regular. Fill it up, please.
She tells the attendant what she wants.

He pumps the gas.

The oil's okay, ma'am.
He checks the oil.

That'll be fifteen dollars.
Here you go.
Then Kate pays him.

25

# Taking a Train

**VERBS**
arrive
buy
follow
get off
get on
hear
put
stand
take (a train)
wait
walk

**NOUNS**
gate
machine
passenger
sign
slot
station
ticket
train
window

**ADJECTIVES**
crowded
other

## For Special Attention

- The train is **crowded**. — There are many people on the train.
- He **has to stand**. — There is no place to sit.
- He **hears his station**. — Someone says the name of his station.
- **other** passengers — passengers who are **not** Tom

Tom buys a ticket from the machine.

Other passengers buy tickets at the ticket window.

Tom puts his ticket into the slot.

He walks through the gate.

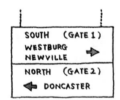

He follows the signs to his gate.

He waits for the train.

His train arrives. He gets on.

The train is crowded. He has to stand.

Tom hears his station.

NEWVILLE STATION

He gets off.

## Key Vocabulary

**VERBS**
check
get in
give
go
hail
pay
start
stop
take (a taxi)
tell

**NOUNS**
directions
driver
fare
meter
taxi
tip

**ADVERB**
where

## For Special Attention

- **hail a taxi** — to wave or signal a taxi to stop
- **give directions** — to tell someone how to get somewhere
- **give a tip** — to give extra money to thank a person
- **check the meter** — to look quickly to see what it says

Pam hails a taxi.

She gets in.

She tells the driver where to go.

He starts the meter.

Pam checks the meter.

She gives directions.

She tells the driver where to stop.

She pays the fare and gives him a tip.

27

# 18 Walking Somewhere

## Key Vocabulary

**VERBS**
cross
go
run
step
stop
trip
wait
walk

**NOUNS**
corner
crack
crosswalk
dirt
overpass
parking lot
puddle
sidewalk
street

**OTHERS**
busy (adj.)
late (adj.)
over (prep.)
sometimes (adv.)
somewhere (adv.)
through (prep.)

## For Special Attention

- **sidewalk** — a place for walking
- an **overpass** — a bridge for passing over a street

Dan walks on the sidewalk.

He steps over dirt and puddles.

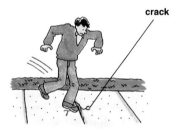

Sometimes he trips on a crack.

He stops at the corner and waits.

Then Dan crosses in the crosswalk.

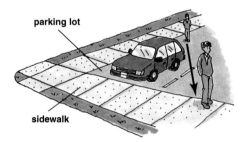

Sometimes he walks through a parking lot.

Sometimes Dan is late. He runs.

He crosses a busy street. He goes over an overpass.

# Riding a Bicycle

## Key Vocabulary

**VERBS**
get off
get on
go
hold
lock
move
pedal
put on
ride
shift
slow down
squeeze

**NOUNS**
bike (bicycle)
brakes
gear
handlebars
helmet
hill
pedal
rack
shift lever

**OTHERS**
lower (adj.)
up (adv.)

## For Special Attention

- **helmet** — a very hard hat
- **pedals** — the parts of the bike for your feet (You **pedal** or push on the pedals.)
- **squeeze** — to hold something tightly
- **shift gears** — to change from one gear to another

I put on my helmet.

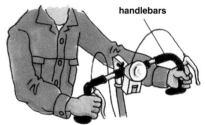
I hold the handlebars.

I get on the bike.

I pedal, and the bike moves.

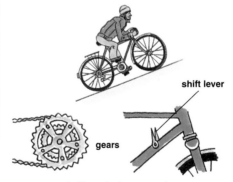
I go up a hill. I shift into a lower gear.

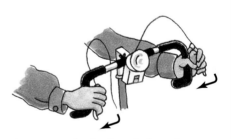
I squeeze the brakes. I slow down.

I get off my bike.

I put it in a bike rack. I lock it.

# 20 Returning Home

## Key Vocabulary

**VERBS**

| | |
|---|---|
| change | pick up |
| check | press |
| choose | put |
| get | put on |
| get off | return |
| get on | take (an elevator) |
| go | take off |
| go back | unlock |
| hang | wait |
| open | walk |

**NOUNS**

| | |
|---|---|
| apartment | hall |
| bag | house |
| building | living room |
| closet | mail |
| clothes | mailbox |
| coat | phone message |
| door | shoe |
| elevator | step |
| floor | |

**OTHERS**

casual (adj.)
home (adv.)
inside (adv.)
work (adj.)

## For Special Attention

- **go back** — return
- **take an elevator** — to use it to get somewhere
- **press** "up" — press the "up" button

## To an Apartment

Dan goes back to his building.

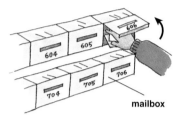

mailbox

He gets his mail.

Then he takes an elevator to his floor.

He walks down the hall.

He opens his door and goes inside.

## Taking an Elevator

Press "up."

Wait for the elevator.

Get on the elevator.

Choose a floor.

Get off the elevator.

**To a House**

I go back to my house.

I walk up the steps.

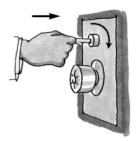
I unlock the door.

I open the door.

I put my bag down.

I hang my coat in the closet.

I take off my shoes.

I pick up my mail.

Then I go into the living room.

I check for phone messages (see p. 72).

Then I change clothes.

I take off my work clothes…

…and put on my casual clothes (see p. 12).

31

# 21 Making a Salad

## Key Vocabulary

**VERBS**
drain
make
mix
pour
put
slice
sprinkle
wash

**NOUNS**
bowl
cheese
cucumber
dressing
grater
lettuce
salad
tomato

**OTHERS**
on top (adverbial)
some (adj.)

## For Special Attention

- **on top** — on the top of something
- **drain** — to let water go off or out of something
- **slice** something — to cut it into thin, flat pieces
- **sprinkle** — to put a small amount over something

Paul washes some lettuce.

He drains it.

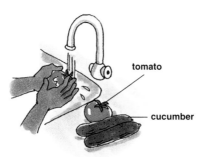

He also washes some tomatoes and cucumbers.

He slices them.

Paul mixes the lettuce and cucumbers in a bowl.

He puts the tomatoes on top.

Then he sprinkles some cheese on the salad.

He pours some dressing on the salad.

# 22 Preparing Vegetables

## Key Vocabulary

**VERBS**
boil
chop
peel
prepare
put
slice
steam
turn on
wash

**NOUNS**
broccoli
burner
carrot
lid
pan
steam
steamer basket
vegetable
water

**ADJECTIVES**
boiling
some

## For Special Attention

- **steam** something — to put food above, not in, boiling water (The steam cooks the food.)
- **slice** something — to cut into thin, flat pieces
- **chop** something — to cut into pieces that are not flat and thin

Kate peels some carrots.

She slices them.

She chops some broccoli.

She washes the broccoli.

Kate puts some water in a pan.

She puts a steamer basket in the pan.

Then she puts the vegetables in the steamer basket.

She puts a lid on the pan. She turns on the burner.

boiling water
steam
The water boils and steams the vegetables.

# 23 Making Spaghetti

## Key Vocabulary

**VERBS**
add
boil
chop
drain
fry
heat
make
pour
pour off
put
start
stir
turn
turn down
turn off

**NOUNS**
beef
burner
butter
can
fat
ground beef
heat
liquid
meat
onion
pan
piece
plate
sauce
solid
spaghetti
spice
sugar
tomato sauce
water

**ADJECTIVES**
boiling
brown
done
large
melted
some

Kate chops an onion.

She fries it with ground beef.

Kate stirs it.

The meat turns brown.
She turns off the burner.

She pours off the fat.

2 cans

She puts two cans of tomato sauce in a pan. She heats it.

## For Special Attention

- **ground beef** — meat from a cow (The meat is ground into small pieces.)
- **fat** — an oily part of meat (It turns to a liquid when you cook the meat.)
- **pour off** — to separate the liquid from a solid; drain the solid
- **turn down the heat** — to turn to a lower heat and let food cook slowly
- **spaghetti** — a kind of pasta

- You often use **spices** to cook. Spices add taste. Oregano and basil are spices for tomato sauce.
- **fry** and **boil**:
  –Kate fries the meat.
  –The meat fries.
  –Kate boils the water.
  –The water boils.
  –The pasta boils in the water.

Kate adds the beef and onions.

She stirs it. She adds some spices.

It starts to boil.

Kate turns down the heat.

In a large pan, she boils some water.

She puts some spaghetti into the boiling water.

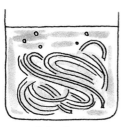

It boils.

The spaghetti is done. Kate drains it.

She puts the spaghetti on a plate. She pours some sauce over it.

## Liquids and Solids
### Some liquids

### Some solids

water

melted butter

tomato sauce

spaghetti

onion

pan

a piece of butter

sugar

# 24 Cooking Rice

## Key Vocabulary

**VERBS**
add
boil
check
clean
cook
eat
get
heat
pour
pour off
put
start
turn down
wait

**NOUNS**
cup
heat
lid
minute
pot
rice
water

**ADJECTIVES**
clean
dirty
ready

## For Special Attention

- **He cleans the rice.** — There are many different types of rice. You need to clean some types. Many Americans do not clean rice.
- **be done** — to be finished (for food, to be cooked)

Paul gets one cup of rice.

He pours it into a pot.

He cleans the rice. He puts water in the pot.

Paul pours off the dirty water.

2 cups

He adds two cups of clean water.

Paul puts a lid on the pot.

He heats the water.

OFF

It starts to boil. He turns down the heat.

Is it done?

He waits 15 minutes. Then he checks the rice.

Yes, done.

It's ready to eat.

# 25  Eating Dinner

## Key Vocabulary

**VERBS**
eat
have
pass
put
set (a table)
sit down
take
talk

**NOUNS**
cup
dessert
dinner
food
fork
glass
knife
lap
napkin
plate
salad
salad bowl
saucer
spoon
table

**ADJECTIVES**
more
some

## For Special Attention

• **lap** — the upper part of your legs when you sit down

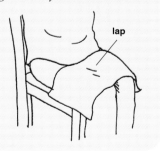
lap

### Paul and Kate Set the Table

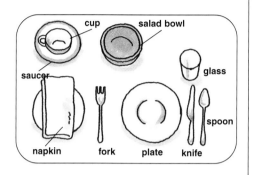

cup    salad bowl
saucer    glass
napkin    fork    plate    knife    spoon

Everyone sits down at the table.

They put their napkins on their laps.

Paul takes some salad.

Pass the salad, please.
He passes the salad to Kate.

Then they take some food.

Where did you go today?
Nowhere special.
They talk.

I want some more spaghetti.
Paul takes more food.

Mmmm.
It's good.
Then they have dessert.

# 26 Clearing the Table

## Key Vocabulary

**VERBS**
carry
clear
cover
put
scrape
stack
take
wipe off

**NOUNS**
crumb
dish
garbage
kitchen
leftovers
plate
refrigerator
serving dish
table

**ADJECTIVE**
done

## For Special Attention

- **Everyone is done.** — Everyone is finished eating.
- **leftovers** — the food you keep after dinner
- **crumbs** — small pieces of food to throw away
- **stack** things — to put things on top of one another

---

Everyone is done. Paul and Kate clear the table.

You stay here.

Paul and I will clean up.

They stack the dishes.

They carry them to the kitchen.

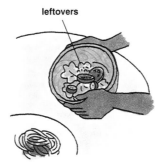

leftovers

They take the serving dishes to the kitchen.

They cover the leftovers.

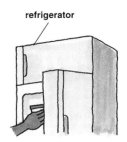

refrigerator

They put them in the refrigerator.

Paul and Kate scrape the plates.

crumbs

They wipe off the table.

They put the crumbs into the garbage.

# Doing Dishes

## Key Vocabulary

**VERBS**
do dishes
drip
dry
go
pull
put
put away
rinse
scrub
wash

**NOUNS**
dish
dish soap
drain
plug
rack
sink
towel
water

**ADJECTIVE**
dirty

## For Special Attention

- **dish soap** — detergent
- **scrub** — to rub very hard and for a long time

Paul puts the plug in the sink.

He puts water in the sink.

He puts dish soap in the water.

Paul washes the dishes.

He scrubs some dirty dishes.

Then he rinses the dishes.

rack

He puts the dishes in the rack.

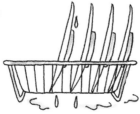

The water drips off them.

Then he pulls the plug from the sink.

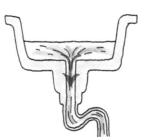

The water goes down the drain.

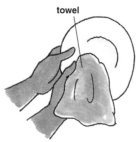

towel

Paul dries the dishes.

Then he puts the dishes away.

# 28 Playing a CD (Compact Disc)

## Key Vocabulary

**VERBS**
come out
eject
go
listen to
make
pick
pick up
play
press in
put
repeat
skip
stop
take out
use
want

**NOUNS**
button        number
case          player
CD            remote
compact disc  track
disc          tray
music

**OTHERS**
back (adv.)
finally (adv.)
forward (adv.)
next (adj.)

## For Special Attention

- **remote** — a remote control
- Each song on a **CD** is a **track**. Each track has a **number.**

I pick a CD.

I take it out of the case.

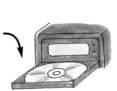
I put the disc into the tray.

I pick up the remote.

I press in the track number I want.

I listen to the music.

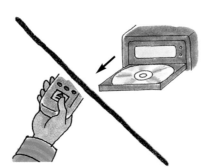
Finally, I eject the CD.

### Using a CD Remote

| Button | What the CD Player Does |
|---|---|
|  PLAY | It plays the CD. |
|  SKIP or NEXT | It goes forward to the next track. |
|  REPEAT or BACK | It goes back a track. |
|  STOP | It stops playing the CD. |
|  EJECT | It makes the CD tray come out. |

# 29 Using a Cassette Player

## Key Vocabulary

**VERBS**
eject
fast-forward
get
go
open
pause
play
plug in
put
put back
put on
rewind
start
stop
take out
turn down
turn up
use

**NOUNS**
beginning
button
case
cassette
earphones
music
player
tape
time

**OTHERS**
back (adv.)    loud (adj.)
done (adj.)    short (adj.)
fast (adv.)    soft (adj.)
forward (adv.)

## For Special Attention

- **louder** — the opposite of **softer**

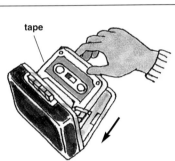

I put a tape into the player.

I plug in the earphones.

I put them on.

I start the tape.

I turn it up. The music gets louder.

I turn it down. The music gets softer.

When I am done, I take the tape out.

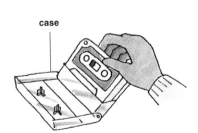

I put it back in the case.

### Using a Casette Player

| Button | What the Cassette Player Does |
|---|---|
|  PLAY | It plays the tape. |
|  FAST-FORWARD | It goes forward fast. |
|  REWIND | It goes back to the beginning. |
|  STOP | It stops the tape. |
|  PAUSE | It stops the tape for a short time. |
|  EJECT | It opens the cassette player. |

# 30 Reading

## Key Vocabulary

**VERBS**
close
find
look at
look through
look up
open
pick up
read
see
turn

**NOUNS**
ad
article
author
book
cover
dictionary
index
magazine
page
part
picture
table of contents
title
word

**ADJECTIVES**
done
interesting
new
some

## For Special Attention

- **look through** — to turn the pages quickly
- **ad** — a short form of "advertisement"
- **look up** a word — to find it in the dictionary

## Reading a Book

Pam opens the book.

She reads. Then she turns the pages.

### Some Parts of a Book

cover
title
author

table of contents

index

Pam sees a new word.

"Bogus"? What does that mean?

She looks it up in a dictionary.

She's done. She closes the book.

## Reading a Magazine

Pam picks up a magazine.

She looks at the ads.

She looks through the magazine.

Pam finds an interesting article.

She reads the article.

picture

She looks at the pictures.

# 31 Watching Television

## Key Vocabulary

**VERBS**
change
go
hear
like
pick up
turn off
turn on
turn up
use
watch

**NOUNS**
channel
commercial
game show
kitchen
news
remote
television
TV
volume

**ADVERBS**
on
over

## For Special Attention

- **TV** — television
- **commercial** — advertising on TV or radio
- **news** — a report about what is happening
- TVs have **channels** or numbers for different programs.
- **remote** — remote control

Tom picks up the remote.

He turns the TV on.

Now, for fifty three dollars, what's the name of...

A game show is on.

Tom doesn't like it.

He uses the remote.

He changes the channel.

Tom can't hear the TV.
He turns up the volume.

A commercial is on.

He goes to the kitchen.

He watches the news.

That's the end of the news.

The news is over.

He turns off the TV.

# 32 Watching a Video

## Key Vocabulary

**VERBS**
eject
leave
pause
put
rent
return
rewind
see
start
stop
switch
take out
turn on
want
watch

**NOUNS**
end
setting
tape
VCR
video

**ADVERBS**
again
later

## For Special Attention

- **rent** something — to pay money to use it for a short time (After you use it, you **return** it or give it back.)
- **video** and **tape** — short forms of "videotape"
- **VCR** — a **V**ideo **C**assette **R**ecorder
- **leave for a minute** — to leave for a short time and then come back
- **pause** — to stop it for a short time

There you are, ma'am.

Jenny rents a video.

She takes the tape out.

She switches to the video setting.

Jenny turns on the VCR.

She puts the video into it.

Then she starts the tape.

Jenny and Tom watch the video.

I'd like to see that again.

They want to see it again. They rewind the tape.

Tom leaves for a minute. Jenny pauses the tape.

At the end, she stops the tape.

She rewinds and ejects it.

Later, she returns the video.

## Key Vocabulary

**VERBS**
babysit
change
do
draw
drop off
pick up
play
put
read
take
take (a bath)
take care of
watch

**NOUNS**
aunt
baby
bath
block
child (children)
cousin
crib
diaper
parent
picture
playground
puzzle
TV
uncle

**OTHERS**
later (adv.)
other (adj.)

## For Special Attention

- **kids** — **children**
- **parents** — father and mother
- Tom's **aunt** is his father's sister. His **uncle** is married to her. His **cousins** are the children of his aunt and uncle.

Tom babysits his cousins. He takes care of them for their parents.

Bye, kids. Be good!
Bye, Aunt Rita.
Tom's aunt and uncle drop the children off.

Tom takes them to a playground.

blocks
They play with blocks.

They draw pictures.

They do a puzzle.

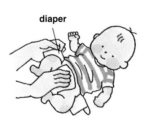
diaper
Tom changes the baby's diaper.

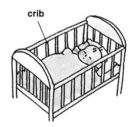
crib
He puts the baby in the crib.

The other children take a bath.

Tom reads to them.

They watch TV.

Come on, kids. Time to go. Thanks, Tom.
Sure. Any time.
Later, their parents pick the children up.

## Key Vocabulary

**VERBS**
brush
change
fall asleep
get into
go
hang up
lie down
pull back
put
read
say good night
set
turn off
turn on
use
wash
yawn

**NOUNS**
alarm clock     laundry basket
bed             light
clothes         nightgown
covers          parent
face            toilet
lamp            tooth (teeth)

**OTHERS**
dirty (adj.)
finally (adv.)
late (adv.)
next to (prep.)
some (adj.)
upstairs (adv.)

## For Special Attention

- **set** her alarm clock — to turn the alarm to the time for it to ring in the morning
- **covers** — the top sheet, blanket, and bedspread

It's late.     Jenny yawns.     She says good night to her parents.

Good night, Jen.

Good night, Mom, Dad.

She goes upstairs.     She changes into her nightgown.

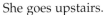

Jenny hangs up some clothes.     She puts her dirty clothes in the laundry basket.

She brushes her teeth.     She washes her face...     ...and uses the toilet.

lamp

Jenny turns on her lamp.

light

She turns off the light.

She pulls back the covers…

…and gets into bed.

She sets her alarm clock.

Jenny puts it next to her lamp.

She reads.

Finally, she turns off the lamp.

She lies down.

She falls asleep.

47

# 35 Doing Laundry

## Key Vocabulary

**VERBS**

| | |
|---|---|
| carry | put in |
| check | rinse |
| do laundry | set |
| dry | sort |
| fold | spin |
| hang out | take |
| hang up | take out of |
| heat | turn on |
| iron | wash |
| put | |
| put away | |

**NOUNS**

clothes
color
detergent
dryer
iron
laundry
laundry basket
machine
pocket
room
thing
washing machine

**OTHERS**

dark (adj.)
light (adj.)
out (adv.)
some (adj.)
wet (adj.)

## For Special Attention

- **laundry** — clothes to be washed
- **sort** — to divide into different groups

I do my laundry.

I carry my laundry basket to the laundry room.

I take the laundry out.

Then I sort the dark colors from the light colors.

I check the pockets.

I take things out of the pockets.

Then I put the laundry into the washing machine.

I set the machine.

Then I put in some detergent.

I turn the machine on.

48

The machine washes,

…rinses,

…and spins the laundry.

I take the wet clothes out.

I hang some laundry
out to dry.

I put some laundry
into the dryer.

The dryer heats
and dries it.

Then I take it out of
the machine.

I fold some things…

…and put them away.

iron

I iron some things…

…and hang them up.

# 36    Cleaning the House

## Key Vocabulary

**VERBS**

| | |
|---|---|
| clean | scrub |
| dust | sweep |
| empty | throw out |
| mop | tie up |
| pick up | vacuum |
| put | wash |
| put out | wipe |

**NOUNS**

| | |
|---|---|
| bag | kitchen |
| bathroom | living room |
| bathtub | mirror |
| bottle | mop |
| broom | newspaper |
| bucket | recycling |
| can | recycling box |
| counter | refrigerator |
| dustpan | sink |
| floor | thing |
| food | toilet |
| garbage | vacuum cleaner |
| house | wastebasket |
| jar | |

**ADJECTIVES**

bad
big
old

## For Special Attention

- **dust** something — to remove the dust from it (Dust is a light kind of dirt.)

### In the Living Room

Pam picks up things.

She dusts…

…and wipes.

vacuum cleaner

Then she vacuums.

### In the Kitchen

refrigerator

Dan cleans the refrigerator.

Yecch! This is bad.

He throws out bad food.

Pam wipes the counters.

broom

She sweeps the floor.

## In the Bathroom

Dan scrubs the toilet.

He cleans the sink.

He scrubs the bathtub.

Dan washes the mirror.

broom

dustpan

Then he sweeps the floor…

mop

bucket

…and mops it.

## Taking Out the Garbage

They tie up old newspapers.

jar    bottle

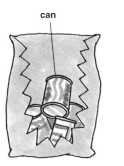

can

They put bottles, cans, and jars into bags.

They put them out for recycling.

recycling box

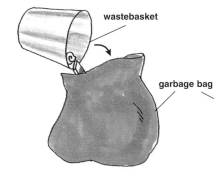

wastebasket

garbage bag

Then they empty wastebaskets…

kitchen garbage

…and the kitchen garbage into a big garbage bag.

They put it in the garbage can.

garbage can

51

# 37 Taking Care of a Cat

## Key Vocabulary

**VERBS**
clean
jump
open
pet
play
purr
put
take care of

**NOUNS**
cat
dish
food
litter box
string
water

**ADJECTIVES**
another
happy
some

## For Special Attention

- **litter box** — where a cat "goes to the bathroom"
- **purr** — the noise a cat makes when it is happy (A cat usually "meows.")
- Most people call their cat "he" or "she," not "it."

Tom opens the cat food.

He puts it in the cat's dish.

He puts some water in another dish.

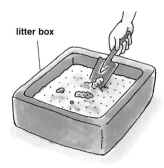

He cleans the litter box.

Tom pets the cat.

The cat purrs. She is happy.

He plays with the cat.

The cat jumps on the string.

52

# 38 Taking Care of a Dog

## Key Vocabulary

**VERBS**
bark
bring back
call
pet
put
take
take care of
throw
wag

**NOUNS**
dish
dog
food
leash
stick
tail
walk
water

**OTHERS**
another (adj.)
later (adv.)
some (adj.)

## For Special Attention

- Most people call their dog "he" or "she," not "it."
- A dog **wags** his tail. He moves his tail back and forth.
- **bark** — a noise a dog makes

I call my dog.

I pet him.

He wags his tail.

He barks.

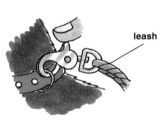

I put some food in his dish.

I put water in another dish.

Later, I put a leash on him.

I take him for a walk.

I throw a stick.

He brings it back.

53

## Key Vocabulary

**VERBS**
push
put
rake
start
take care of
trim
water

**NOUNS**
compost pile
gas
grass
hose
lawn
mower
rake
seed
tree

**OTHERS**
back and forth (adverbial)
some (adj.)

## For Special Attention

- **mower** — a machine that cuts grass
- **compost pile** — old leaves, grass, and twigs
- **Grass seed** grows to become grass.
- **water the lawn** — to put water on the grass
- **lawn** — the area near a house where grass grows

Pam puts gas in her lawn mower.

Vroom!

She starts the mower.

She pushes the mower back and forth.

She trims the grass by the tree.

rake

Pam rakes the grass.

compost pile

She puts it on the compost pile.

She puts some grass seed on the lawn.

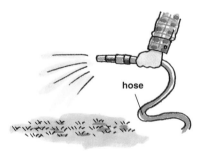

hose

Then she waters the lawn.

## Key Vocabulary

**VERBS**
check for
cover
cut
pick
plant
put
spray
take care of
tie
turn
water
weed

**NOUNS**
fertilizer
flower
garden
gardening
hose
insect
insecticide

leaves
plant
seed
seedling
soil
stake

**OTHERS**
extra (adj.)
finally (adv.)
some (adj.)

## For Special Attention

- **seedling** — a very young plant
- **weed** a garden — to pull out the plants you don't want
- **insects** — small animals with six legs (They often eat plants.)
- **fertilizer** — something that makes the soil better for plants
- **check for** — to look for something

### Planting a Garden

Tom turns the soil.

He plants some seeds.

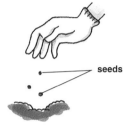

He covers them with soil.

Tom plants some seedlings.

He ties them to stakes.

Then he waters the garden.

### Taking Care of a Garden

Tom weeds the garden.

He cuts extra leaves from some plants.

He checks for insects.

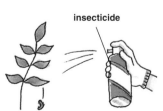

Tom sprays some plants.

He puts fertilizer on the soil.

Finally, he picks some flowers.

## Key Vocabulary

**VERBS**
clean
dry
get
put
rinse
shine
vacuum
wash
wipe off

**NOUNS**
car
dashboard
floor
inside
outside
sponge
water
wax
window

**OTHERS**
finally (adv.)
soapy (adj.)
some (adj.)

## For Special Attention

- **wax** — something that makes a car shine

### Inside

I wash the windows.

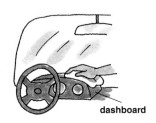

dashboard

I wipe off the dashboard.

I vacuum the floor.

### Outside

sponge

soapy water

I get some soapy water.

I wash the car.

I rinse the car.

I dry the car.

Then I put wax on it.

The wax dries.

I wipe the wax off.

Then I shine the car.

Finally, I wash the outside of the windows.

## Key Vocabulary

**VERBS**
ask for
call
check
come back
give
take
tell
work on

**NOUNS**
appointment
bill
car
cost
estimate
garage
mechanic
repair

**ADVERB**
later

## For Special Attention

- **for repairs** — for work to correct problems
- **estimate** — a guess about an amount of money
- **call for an appointment** — to telephone someone and set a time when you can meet
- **"Ouch!"** — something people say when they are hurt or when they are surprised by something they don't like or by something unpleasant

I call the garage for an appointment.

I take my car to the garage.

The mechanic checks the car.

I ask for an estimate. He tells me the cost.

He works on the car.

I come back later for the car.

He gives me the bill.

## Key Vocabulary

**VERBS**
change
have (has)
jack up
lower
put on
take off
take out
tighten

**NOUNS**
car
hubcap
nut
tire
trunk
wrench

**OTHERS**
by hand (adverbial)
finally (adv.)
flat (adj.)
some (adj.)
spare (adj.)

## For Special Attention

• a **spare** thing — something extra that you don't usually need
• You can **jack something up.** You cannot "jack it down." You lower it.
• A **nut** goes on a bolt. (See p. 61.)

My car has a flat tire. I change it.

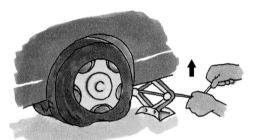

I jack the car up.

I take off the flat tire.

I take out the spare tire.

I put on the spare tire.

I tighten the nuts by hand.

I lower the car.

I tighten the nuts some more with a wrench.

Finally, I put the hubcap on.

# 44  Dealing with a Power Failure

## Key Vocabulary

**VERBS**
come on
deal with
find
go out
light
reset
turn on

**NOUNS**
box
breaker
candle
circuit breaker
failure
flashlight
power
sister
storm

**OTHERS**
back (adv.)
off (adv.)
some (adj.)

## For Special Attention

- **power** — electric power
- **Circuit breakers** look like switches. They turn off if there is too much electric power. Some houses have fuses instead of circuit breakers.
- **breaker** — circuit breaker
- to **deal with** — to do the right things when there is a problem

There's a storm.

Our power goes out.

I turn on a flashlight.

My sister lights some candles.

We find the circuit-breaker box.

Some breakers are off.

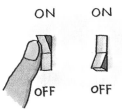

We reset them.

The power comes back on.

## Key Vocabulary

**VERBS**
cut
join
make
mark
measure
sand
trim
work

**NOUNS**
glue
hammer
nail
piece
place
plane
ruler
sandpaper
saw
screw
screwdriver
wood

**ADJECTIVE**
smooth

## For Special Attention

- You use a **hammer** with **nails.**
- **join** things — to put them together
- Some things you can use to measure:
  **ruler** — This is usually twelve inches long.
  **yardstick** — This is one yard (thirty-six inches) long.
  **tape measure** — This can measure longer distances.

First, you measure the wood.

You mark the places to cut.

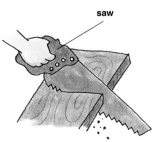

Then you cut with a saw.

You trim wood with a plane.

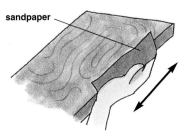

You sand the wood. That makes it smooth.

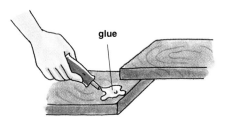

You can join two pieces with glue,

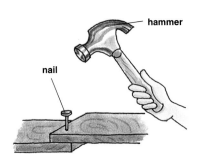

...with nails,

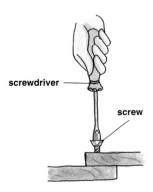

...or with screws.

## Key Vocabulary

**VERBS**
bolt
drill
hold
join
loosen
put
tighten
turn

**NOUNS**
bolt
drill
hole
nut
pliers
screw
screwdriver
thing
top
washer
wrench

**OTHERS**
by hand (adverbial)
clockwise (adv.)
counterclockwise (adv.)
some (adj.)
through (prep.)

## For Special Attention

- **Pliers** always has an "s."
- **clockwise** — the direction that the hands of a clock move
- **counterclockwise** — the opposite of clockwise; the opposite direction the hands of a clock move
- You **drill** holes with a **drill.** You **bolt** things with **bolts,** and **screw** them with **screws.**

### To Bolt Things

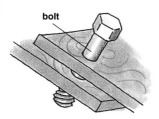

You put a bolt through some holes.

You put a washer onto the bolt.

You tighten a nut by hand.

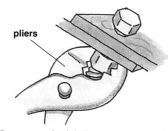

Then you hold the nut with pliers.

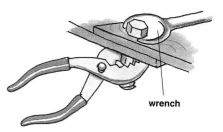

You tighten the bolt with a wrench.

### To Join Things with Screws

You drill a hole.

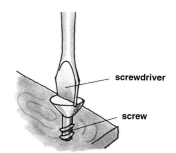

You put a screwdriver into the top of the screw.

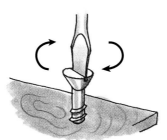

You turn the screwdriver clockwise.

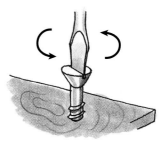

To loosen the screw, you turn it counterclockwise.

## Key Vocabulary

**VERBS**

| | |
|---|---|
| check | shop |
| choose | smell |
| get | take |
| go | use |
| look for | weigh |
| put | |

**NOUNS**

aisle
bag
basket
can
cart
checkout counter
cheese
chicken
cold cut
deli
fruit
groceries
list
meat
milk
pizza
pound
price
shopper
special
toilet paper
vegetable

**OTHERS**

another (adj.)
cheap (adj.)
finally (adv.)
frozen (adj.)
shopping (adj.)
some (adj.)

Tom gets a shopping cart.

Another shopper uses a shopping basket.

Tom checks his list.

He checks the fruit and vegetables.

He smells them.

He puts some fruit in a bag.

He weighs the fruit.

## For Special Attention

- **Cold cuts** are cooked meats that you eat cold in a sandwich.
- **check** a list — to look at it quickly
- Tom **checks** the fruit. He looks at it and smells it to see if it's good.

- **on special** — for a lower price than usual (The lower price is called a **special**.)

Next, Tom gets some meat.

At the deli, he gets some cold cuts…

…and cheese.

Tom goes through the aisles.

He checks the prices.

He chooses the cheaper can.

He looks for specials.

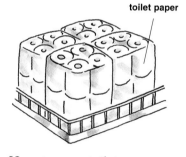

He gets some toilet paper.

He gets some milk.

Tom takes some frozen pizza.

Finally, he goes to the checkout counter.

# 48  Paying for Things

## Key Vocabulary

**VERBS**

| | |
|---|---|
| ask | ring up |
| count | scan |
| give | sign |
| pay | swipe |
| press | take out |
| print | tell |
| put | write |
| record | |

**NOUNS**

| | |
|---|---|
| bar code | key |
| card | money |
| cash | payment slip |
| cashier | purchase |
| change | receipt |
| check | register |
| checkbook | thing |
| copy | total |
| credit card | |
| ID (identification) | |

**ADJECTIVE**

some

## For Special Attention

- **ring something up** — to make a machine record a price
- A machine **scans** a bar code by shining light on it.
- The money I give the cashier is more than the total price. The difference is my **change**.
- a **bar code** — dark bars that tell the price of something
- **ID** — identification (A driver's license, passport, or employee card can be used for ID.)
- **swipe** — to pass a credit card through a machine

---

The cashier rings up Tom's purchases.

She scans bar codes.

She presses keys on the cash register.

She tells him the total.

> That'll be $23.50.

---

### Paying with Cash

Tom takes some money out.

He gives it to the cashier.

> Here's $30.

She puts it into the cash register.

She takes out the change.

She counts it.

> $23.50, 24, 25 and 5 makes $30.

She gives it to Tom with the receipt.

64

## Paying by Check

Tom writes a check.

FIRST SAVINGS BANK      4731

TOM JOHNSON
1215 PIEM DR.
WEST MOSES, WI
53717

JULY 17, 2003

TO THE ORDER OF    SUPER Y MART    $ 23.50

TWENTY-THREE AND 50/100 DOLLARS

☐☐1743411      SIGNATURE

He signs the check.

Can I see some ID, please?

Sure. Here's my driver's license.

The cashier asks for some ID.

He records the check in his checkbook.

Thank you.

Thanks. Bye.

She gives him his ID and a receipt.

## Paying by Credit Card

Tom gives his card to the cashier.

She swipes the card.

A payment slip is printed.

Tom signs the payment slip.

Then she gives him a copy,

...the receipt, and his card back.

## Key Vocabulary

**VERBS**
check
endorse
fill out
give
give back
go
print
write

**NOUNS**

| | |
|---|---|
| account | deposit slip |
| amount | number |
| bank | passbook |
| cash | teller |
| check | total |
| deposit | |

**ADJECTIVE**
total

## For Special Attention

- **account** — the bank's record of how much money a person has in the bank
- **deposit** — money you put in the bank
- **deposit slip** — a bank form to be filled out when putting money in the bank
- **fill out** — to write information in the spaces on a form
- Paul uses a **passbook** at his bank. Some banks send people a statement every month to tell them how much is in their accounts.
- **teller** — a bank worker who helps people put money into their accounts and take it out
- **endorse** — to sign your name on the back of a check

Paul goes to the bank.

He fills out a deposit slip.

FIRST SAVINGS BANK                    DEPOSIT SLIP

Date  April 8, 2003              Cash   45 0 0

| Branch Name | |
|---|---|
| Account Number | 4 1 9 3 1 7 8 |
| Paid by | |

Checks  140
$  192 89

Paul writes his account number, his cash and checks, and the total.

He goes to the teller.

He endorses the checks.

Then he gives the teller his deposit.

The teller checks the amounts.

| Transaction | Amount | Balance |
|---|---|---|
| Carried forward | | 1221.64 |
| Deposit | 192.89 | 1414.53 |

She prints the total amount in Paul's passbook.

Thanks. Have a nice day!

Then she gives him back his passbook.

## Key Vocabulary

**VERBS**
ask
enter
give
go
line up
need
press
put
return
take out
use

**NOUNS**
amount
ATM
card
key
machine
money
PIN
strip

## For Special Attention

- **"Oops!"** — something people say when they realize they made a mistake
- **ATM** — an **A**utomated **T**eller **M**achine (Another name for it is "cash machine.")
- **cash** — money in the form of paper notes and coins (not checks)
- **PIN** — a **P**ersonal **I**dentification **N**umber
- **strip** — the dark magnetic bar on the back of an ATM card
- You **enter** a number by typing it into a machine.

Oops! Where is a cash machine?

Kate needs money.

So she goes to an ATM.

ATM card

She takes out her ATM card.

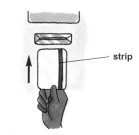

strip

She lines up the strip.

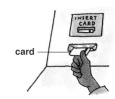

card

She puts the card into the ATM.

keys

PLEASE ENTER YOUR PIN NUMBER

The ATM asks for her PIN.

Kate enters her PIN.
She presses keys.

AMOUNT NEEDED?

She enters the amount of money.

INSERT CARD

TAKE YOUR CARD

The machine returns her card.

PLEASE TAKE YOUR CASH

It gives Kate her money.

# 51 Making a Phone Call

## Key Vocabulary

**VERBS**
answer
dial
hear
look up
make
pick up
ring
say hello
talk

**NOUNS**
call
dial tone
number
phone

## For Special Attention

- **phone** — a short way of saying "telephone"
- Most telephones are push-button phones—you **dial** by pushing buttons.
- **dial tone** — a sound that tells you the phone is ready to use

Jenny looks up Kate's phone number.

Jenny picks up the phone.

Hmmm...

She hears a dial tone.

Then she dials the number.

ring...
ring...

She hears the phone ringing.

Hello?

Kate answers.

Hi, Kate.
This is Jenny.

Jenny says hello.

How are you?

She talks to Kate.

# 52 Answering a Telephone

## Key Vocabulary

**VERBS**
answer
apologize
call
hang up
hear
know
listen
pick up
ring
say hello
talk
tell

**NOUNS**
person
phone
telephone
wrong number

## For Special Attention

• The person who answers a
phone usually speaks first.

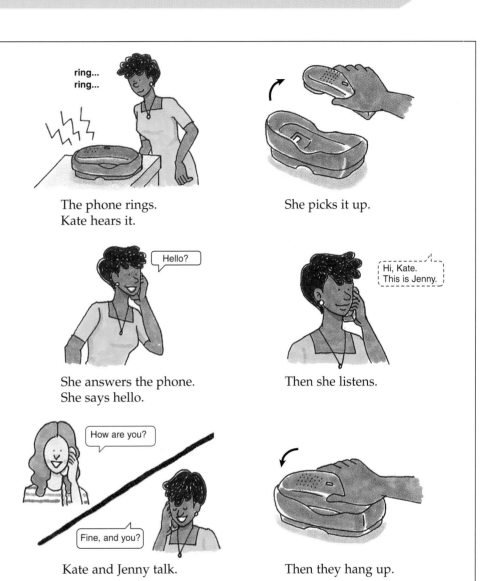

The phone rings.
Kate hears it.

She picks it up.

She answers the phone.
She says hello.

Then she listens.

Kate and Jenny talk.

Then they hang up.

### If It's a Wrong Number:

Someone calls Kate. She
doesn't know the person.

She tells him it's
the wrong number.

He apologizes and
hangs up.

# 53 Leaving a Message

## Key Vocabulary

**VERBS**
ask for
ask to
call
leave
repeat
say
speak
spell

**NOUNS**
last name
message
name
phone number

## For Special Attention

- **leave a message** — to tell it to the person who takes the message
- **repeat** something — to say it again
- Alex Rivera's first name is "Alex." His last name is "Rivera."

I say my name. I ask for Dan.

He isn't there.

I ask to leave a message.

She asks me to repeat my name.

I repeat it.

I spell my last name.

I say my phone number.

I ask for Dan to call me.

# 54

# Taking a Message

## Key Vocabulary

**VERBS**
answer
ask for
call back
get
leave
offer
put
take
write

**NOUNS**
caller
message
phone

**ADVERBS**
later
there

## For Special Attention

- The caller **leaves a message** for Dan with Pam.
- **return a call** — to call back someone who leaves a message for you
- Pam offers to take a message by saying, "Can I take a message?" Another way to say this is: "May I take a message?"

Pam answers the phone.

The caller asks for Dan.

Dan isn't there. Pam offers to take a message.

The caller leaves a message.

Pam writes the message.

She puts it next to the phone.

Later, Dan gets the message.

He calls back.

# 55 Using an Answering Machine

## Key Vocabulary

**VERBS**
call
erase
get home
hear
leave (a message)
listen to
play (a message)
press
record
see
take (notes)
use

**NOUNS**
answering machine
button
message
message light
notes

**ADJECTIVES**
some

## For Special Attention

- **record (a message)** — to put a message on a tape
- **erase (a message)** — to take a message off a tape
- **message light** — a light that tells you there is a message

Tom records a message on his answering machine.

Jenny calls. She hears the message.

She leaves a message for Tom.

Tom gets home. He sees a message light.

He presses the button to play the message.

He listens to it...

...and he takes some notes.

Then he erases the message.

## Key Vocabulary

**VERBS**
answer
ask
look at
sign
start
take out
tell
write

**NOUNS**
closing
date
friend
greeting
letter
paper
question

**OTHERS**
myself (pron.)
personal (adj.)
some (adj.)

## For Special Attention

- A **personal letter** is a letter to a friend or family member. It is different from a business letter.
- The **greeting** in a letter usually starts with "Dear" (Dear Mom, Dear Jim).
- The **closing** of a letter comes just before your signature.

I take out some paper to write to my friend.

I write the date and a greeting.

I start to write.

I tell about myself.

I look at her letter to me.

I answer her questions.

I ask questions.

Then I write a closing…

…and sign the letter.

## Key Vocabulary

**VERBS**

| | |
|---|---|
| ask | seal |
| buy | stick |
| fold | take |
| go | wait |
| mail | weigh |
| need | write |
| put | |

**NOUNS**

| | |
|---|---|
| address | middle |
| clerk | picture |
| envelope | post office |
| friend | postage |
| left | stamp |
| letter | turn |
| mailbox | window |

**OTHERS**

express (adj.)
in line (adverbial)
regular (adj.)
some (adj.)
upper (adj.)

## For Special Attention

- **wait in line** — wait for your turn to be served
- You need to **stick** stamps on an envelope. Some stamps need to be moistened and some are already sticky.
- When clerks ask **"Regular** mail or **express?"** they want to know if the letter should be delivered fast.
- **express mail** — mail that goes fast, but costs more
- **regular mail** — usual or normal mail
- **weigh** the letter — to find out how heavy it is and how much it costs

I put some pictures in the envelope.

I fold my letter.

I put it in the envelope with the pictures.

I write my friend's address in the middle of the envelope. I write my address in the upper left.

I seal the envelope.

I take the letter to the post office.

74

I wait in line.

Then it's my turn.

I go to the window.

I ask how much postage I need.

The clerk asks if the letter is regular or express.

He weighs the letter.

I buy stamps.

I stick the stamps on the envelope.

I put the letter in the mailbox.

# 58 Going to a Birthday Party

## Key Vocabulary

**VERBS**
blow out
eat
give
go
light
open
sign
sing
wrap

**NOUNS**
birthday party
cake
candle
card
friend
ice cream
party
present

**ADJECTIVE**
happy

## For Special Attention

- **present** — a gift for a special occasion (a birthday, Christmas, etc.)
- You **wrap** a present in special paper.
- **open** a present — to take off the paper
- **light** a candle — to make it burn
- **blow out** a candle — to make the fire stop burning

Before the party, I wrap a present for my friend…

…and sign a card.

Here, Leo. Happy birthday.

Thanks, Alex. Come on in.

At the party, I give him the present and the card.

candle

Someone lights the candles.

Happy Birthday Dear Leo…

We sing "Happy Birthday."

Leo blows out the candles.

Hey, I like this CD! Thanks.

He opens his presents.

Then everyone eats cake and ice cream.

## Key Vocabulary

**VERBS**
give
go to
greet
have dinner
introduce
say good night
say hello
shake hands
talk
thank

**NOUNS**
dinner
dinner party
guest
host
people
wine

**OTHERS**
inside (adv.)
later (adv.)
other (adj.)
some (adj.)

## For Special Attention

• In the United States, it's polite for a guest at an adult party to bring some wine, flowers, or a small gift to the host.

Dan (the host) greets Tom and Jenny (the guests).

They give him some wine.

Inside, they say hello to other people.

Dan introduces Tom and Jenny to some people.

They shake hands…

…and talk.

They have dinner.

Later, the guests say good night and thank Dan.

## Key Vocabulary

**VERBS**
buy
choose
go
leave
see
tear
watch

**NOUNS**
movie
popcorn
preview
seat
ticket
ticket-taker

**OTHERS**
at the end (adverbial)
some (adj.)

## For Special Attention

• **preview** — a small part of something you can see completely later

We choose a movie.

> Fourteen dollars, please.

> Two please, for *Skull Night.*

We buy tickets…

> Two large popcorns, please.

> Okay.

…and some popcorn.

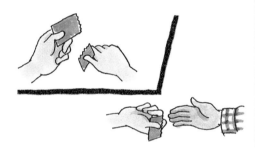

The ticket-taker tears our tickets.

We go to our seats.

COMING SOON

We watch the previews.

SKULL NIGHT

Then we see the movie.

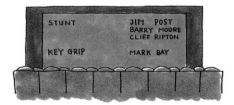

STUNT          JIM POST
               BARRY MOORE
               CLIFF RIPTON

KEY GRIP       MARK BAY

At the end, we leave.

## Key Vocabulary

**VERBS**
eat
get
give
order
pay
read
take
throw out
wait

**NOUNS**
clerk
drink
fast food
food
lunch
menu
napkin
people
restaurant
straw
trash

**OTHERS**
finished (adj.)
in line (adverbial)
some (adj.)

## For Special Attention

- In a fast food restaurant, the **menu** is usually on a large board on the wall.
- Jenny orders her food **"for here."** She eats it in the restaurant.
- People who get their food **"to go"** eat it outside the restaurant.

Jenny waits in line.

She reads the menu.

One Big Burger, some fries, and a cola, please.

For here, please.

For here or to go?

She orders her food and a drink.

That'll be five-twenty.

Right.

The clerk gives Jenny the food. Jenny pays her.

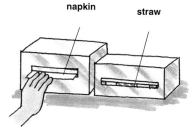

napkin    straw

Jenny takes some napkins and a straw.

She eats her lunch.

Other people get their food to go.

THANK YOU

Jenny is finished. She throws out the trash.

# Common Measurements, Days, Months, and Numbers

|  | American | Metric |
|---|---|---|
| **Weight** | 1 pound [1 lb.] (16 ounces) | 0.45 kilogram (kg) |
|  | 1 ounce [1 oz.] | 28.35 grams (g) |
| **Distance** | 1 mile [1 mi.] (5,280 feet) | 1.609 kilometers (km) |
|  | 1 yard [1 yd.] (3 feet) | 0.914 meter (m) |
|  | 1 foot [1 ft. or 1'] (12 inches) | 0.3048 meter (m) |
|  | 1 inch [1 in. or 1"] | 2.54 centimeters (cm) |
| **Volume/Capacity** | 1 gallon [1 gal.] (4 quarts) | 3.785 liters (l) |
|  | 1 quart [1 qt.] (2 pints) | 0.946 liter (l) |
|  | 1 pint [1 pt.] (2 cups) | 0.473 liter (l) |
|  | 1 cup [1 c.] (8 fluid ounces) | 236.6 milliliters (ml) |
|  | 1 fluid ounce [1 fl. oz.] | 29.57 milliliters (ml) |

## Temperature

F = Fahrenheit     C = Celsius

| | |
|---|---|
| 212°F | 100°C |
| 90°F | 32°C |
| 75°F | 24°C |
| 50°F | 10°C |
| 32°F | 0°C |
| 0°F | -18°C |
| | |

## U.S. Money

One dollar = 100 cents

| Amount | Other names for it |
|---|---|
| 1,000 dollars | a grand |
| 1 dollar | a buck |
| 50 cents | a half-dollar, half a buck |
| 25 cents | a quarter |
| 10 cents | a dime |
| 5 cents | a nickel |
| 1 cent | a penny |

## Days of the Week

Sunday
Monday
Tuesday
Wednesday
Thursday
Friday
Saturday

## Months of the Year

| | |
|---|---|
| January | July |
| February | August |
| March | September |
| April | October |
| May | November |
| June | December |

## Numbers

| | | | |
|---|---|---|---|
| 0 zero | 10 ten | 20 twenty | 30 thirty |
| 1 one | 11 eleven | 21 twenty-one | 40 forty |
| 2 two | 12 twelve | 22 twenty-two | 50 fifty |
| 3 three | 13 thirteen | 23 twenty-three | 60 sixty |
| 4 four | 14 fourteen | 24 twenty-four | 70 seventy |
| 5 five | 15 fifteen | 25 twenty-five | 80 eighty |
| 6 six | 16 sixteen | 26 twenty-six | 90 ninety |
| 7 seven | 17 seventeen | 27 twenty-seven | 100 one hundred |
| 8 eight | 18 eighteen | 28 twenty-eight | 200 two hundred |
| 9 nine | 19 nineteen | 29 twenty-nine | 1,000 one thousand |

# Index

**The terms indexed are all those appearing in captions, labels, and headings in the main text. Explanatory vocabulary from the For Special Attention sections is not indexed.**

The index does not include:
- determiners (a, the, any, each, possessives, etc.)
- personal pronouns
- universal/partitive pronouns (everyone, anyone, something, etc.)
- most prepositions
- conjunctions
- proper names of characters (Tom, Jenny, etc.)

## Part-of-speech Codes

Part-of-speech codes are given if:
- the term appears as more than one part of speech in this volume, or
- the term appears as more than one part of speech in everyday English use; the code specifies which parts of speech can be found in this volume.

## Part-of-speech Codes Used in the Index

| | | |
|---|---|---|
| n. - noun | adj. - adjective | prep. - preposition |
| v. - verb | adv. - adverb | adv'l. - adverbial |

For ease of reference:
- common phrases (e.g., *say good-bye, by hand*) are listed as such
- some past participles of verbs (e.g., *frozen, done*) are listed as adjectives
- some gerunds (e.g., *closing, recycling*) are listed as nouns
- a noun that must be plural in a given meaning is listed in the plural

Otherwise, terms are usually listed in their "base forms"—nouns in the singular, verbs in the infinitive, adjectives and adverbs in the positive.

## Meaning Clues

Meaning clues are given:
- to distinguish various meanings for the term in this volume, or
- if in common use, the expression represents various meanings; the clue specifies which meaning can be found in this volume.

For some terms, the meaning clue is an association with an object that a verb commonly takes or some expression with which the term is commonly used. Such clues include ellipsis points (…).

Unavoidably, some meaning clues will be unclear to beginners using this book. The clues are nonetheless useful because an instructor or a more advanced learner can use them to direct the beginner's attention to the proper point in the text.

# INDEX

## A

account (n.) .......................... .66
ad (n.) .............................. .42
add (v.) ................. .15, 34, 35, 36
address (n.) ......................... .74
again (adv.) ......................... .44
ahead (adv.) ......................... .24
aisle (n.) ........................... .63
alarm clock (n.) ................... .6, 47
amount (n.) ...................... .66, 67
another (adj.) ............. .52, 53, 62
   (see also *other*)
answer (v.) ............... .68, 69, 71, 73
answering machine (n.) .............. .72
   (see also *machine*)
apartment (n.) ...................... .30
apologize (v.) ....................... .69
appointment (n.) .................... .57
arm (n.) ............................ .9
arrive (v.) ...................... .20, 26
article (n.) ......................... .42
asleep (see *fall asleep*)
ask (v.) ................. .65, 67, 73, 75
ask for (v.) .................. .57, 70, 71
ask to (v.) .......................... .70
at the end (adv'l.) .................. .78
ATM (n.) ............................ .67
attendant (n.) ...................... .25
aunt (n.) ........................... .45
author (n.) ......................... .42

## B

baby (n.) ........................... .45
babysit (v.) ......................... .45
back (adv.) .............. .40, 41, 59, 66
   (see also *give back, put back,
   back and forth, back out of*)
back and forth (adv'l.) ............ .8, 54
back out of (v.) ..................... .22
   (see also *back, out*)
backpack (n.) ....................... .19
bacon (n.) .......................... .18
bad (adj.) .......................... .50
bag (n.) ...................... .31, 51, 62
banana (n.) ......................... .16
bank (n.) ........................... .66
bar code (n.) ....................... .64
barefoot (see *go barefoot*)
bark (v.) ........................... .53
basket (n.) ......................... .62
   (see also *laundry basket, steamer basket,
   wastebasket*)
bath (n.) ........................... .45
bathroom (n.) ..................... .6, 51
   (see also *room*)

bathtub (n.) ........................ .51
become (v.) ......................... .15
bed (n.) ...................... .14, 46, 47
bedspread (n.) ...................... .14
beef (n.) ........................... .35
   (see also *ground beef*)
beginning (n.) ...................... .41
behind (prep.) ...................... .22
belt (n.) ........................... .11
   (see also *seat belt*)
between (prep.) ...................... .8
big (adj.) .......................... .51
bike (bicycle) (n.) .................. .29
bill (n.) ........................... .57
birthday party (n.) ................. .76
blanket (n.) ........................ .14
block (n.) .......................... .45
blouse (n.) ......................... .12
blow-dryer (n.) ...................... .9
blow out (v.) ....................... .76
   (see also *out*)
boil (v.) ................. .15, 33, 35, 36
boiling (adj.) .................. .33, 35
bolt (n.) ........................... .61
bolt (v.) ........................... .61
book (n.) ........................... .42
boot (n.) ........................... .13
bottle (n.) ......................... .51
bottom (adj.) ....................... .14
bowl (n.) ..................... .16, 18, 32
   (see also *salad bowl*)
box (n.) ...................... .16, 21, 59
   (see also *litter box, mailbox*)
bra (n.) ............................ .12
brake (n.) ...................... .23, 29
bread (n.) .......................... .16
breaker (n.) ........................ .59
breakfast (n.) .................. .7, 18
bring back (v.) ..................... .53
broccoli (n.) ....................... .33
broom (n.) ...................... .50, 51
brown (adj.) ........................ .34
brush (v.) .................... .7, 8, 46
bucket (n.) ......................... .51
buckle (n.) ......................... .11
buckle (v.) ..................... .11, 22
building (n.) ....................... .30
burner (n.) ................... .17, 33, 34
bus (n.) ...................... .20, 21
busy (adj.) ......................... .28
butter (n.) .................. .16, 17, 35
button (n.) ............. .11, 21, 40, 41, 72
button (v.) ......................... .11
buy (v.) ..................... .26, 75, 78
by hand (adv'l.) ................. .58, 61

## C

cake (n.) ........................... .76
call (n.) ........................... .68
call (v.) ............. .53, 57, 69, 70, 72
call back (v.) ...................... .71

caller (n.) ......................... .71
can (n.) ..................... .34, 51, 63
candle (n.) ..................... .59, 76
cap (n.) ............................ .12
car (n.) ............ .22, 23, 24, 56, 57, 58
card (n.) ............... .21, 65, 67, 76
   (see also *credit card*)
carrot (n.) ......................... .33
carry (v.) ...................... .38, 48
cart (n.) ........................... .62
case (n.) ....................... .40, 41
cash (n.) ....................... .64, 66
cashier (n.) .................... .64, 65
cassette (n.) ....................... .41
casual (adj.) ................... .12, 31
cat (n.) ............................ .52
CD (n.) ............................ .40
   (see also *compact disc*)
cereal (n.) ..................... .16, 18
change (n.) ......................... .64
change (v.) .......... .25, 31, 43, 45, 46, 58
channel (n.) ........................ .43
cheap (adj.) ........................ .63
check (n.) ...................... .65, 66
check (v.) 20, 25, 27, 31, 36, 48, 57, 62, 63, 66
check for (v.) ...................... .55
checkbook (n.) ...................... .65
checkout counter (n.) ............... .63
cheese (n.) ..................... .32, 63
chicken (n.) ........................ .63
child (children) (n.) ............... .45
choose (v.) ............. .10, 30, 63, 78
chop (v.) ....................... .33, 34
circuit breaker (n.) ................ .59
clean (adj.) ........................ .36
clean (v.) ............. .36, 50, 51, 52, 56
clear (v.) .......................... .38
clerk (n.) ...................... .75, 79
clock (n.) .......................... .47
   (see also *alarm clock*)
clockwise (adv.) .................... .61
close (v.) ...................... .9, 42
closet (n.) ......................... .31
closing (n.) ........................ .73
clothes (n.) ........... .12, 13, 31, 46, 49
clutch (n.) ......................... .23
coat (n.) ....................... .13, 31
coffee (n.) ..................... .15, 18
coffeemaker (n.) .................... .15
coffeepot (n.) ...................... .15
cold (adj.) ..................... .13, 16
cold cut (n.) ....................... .63
collar (n.) ......................... .11
color (n.) .......................... .48
come back (v.) ...................... .57
come on (v.) ........................ .59
come out (v.) ....................... .40
commercial (n.) ..................... .43
compact disc (n.) ................... .40
   (see also *CD, disc*)
compost pile (n.) ................... .54
cook (v.) ........................... .36

copy (n.) . . . . . . . . . . . . . . . . . . . . . . . . .65
corner (n.) . . . . . . . . . . . . . . . . . . . . . . . .28
cost (n.) . . . . . . . . . . . . . . . . . . . . . . . . . .57
count (v.) . . . . . . . . . . . . . . . . . . . . . . . . .64
counter (n.) . . . . . . . . . . . . . . . . . . . . . . .50
counterclockwise (adv.) . . . . . . . . . . . . . .61
cousin (n.) . . . . . . . . . . . . . . . . . . . . . . . .45
cover (n.) . . . . . . . . . . . . . . . . . . . . . . . . .42
cover (v.) . . . . . . . . . . . . . . . . . . . . . . .38, 55
covers (n.) . . . . . . . . . . . . . . . . . . . . . . . .47
crack (n.) . . . . . . . . . . . . . . . . . . . . . . . . .28
credit card (n.) . . . . . . . . . . . . . . . . . . . . .65
crib (n.) . . . . . . . . . . . . . . . . . . . . . . . . . .45
cross (v.) . . . . . . . . . . . . . . . . . . . . . . . . .28
crosswalk (n.) . . . . . . . . . . . . . . . . . . . . .28
crowded (adj.) . . . . . . . . . . . . . . . . . . . . .26
crumb (n.) . . . . . . . . . . . . . . . . . . . . . . . .38
cucumber (n.) . . . . . . . . . . . . . . . . . . . . .32
cup (n.) . . . . . . . . . . . . . . . . . . . . . . . .36, 37
     (see also *teacup*)
curtain (n.) . . . . . . . . . . . . . . . . . . . . . . . .9
cut (v.) . . . . . . . . . . . . . . . . . . . . . . . . .55, 60

## D

dark (adj.) . . . . . . . . . . . . . . . . . . . . . .23, 48
dashboard (n.) . . . . . . . . . . . . . . . . . . . . .56
date (n.) . . . . . . . . . . . . . . . . . . . . . . . . . .73
deal with (v.) . . . . . . . . . . . . . . . . . . . . . .59
deli (n.) . . . . . . . . . . . . . . . . . . . . . . . . . .63
deodorant (n.) . . . . . . . . . . . . . . . . . . . . . .9
deposit (n.) . . . . . . . . . . . . . . . . . . . . . . .66
deposit slip (n.) . . . . . . . . . . . . . . . . . . . .66
dessert (n.) . . . . . . . . . . . . . . . . . . . . . . . .37
detergent (n.) . . . . . . . . . . . . . . . . . . . . . .48
dial (v.) . . . . . . . . . . . . . . . . . . . . . . . . . .68
dial tone (n.) . . . . . . . . . . . . . . . . . . . . . .68
diaper (n.) . . . . . . . . . . . . . . . . . . . . . . . .45
dictionary (n.) . . . . . . . . . . . . . . . . . . . . .42
dinner (n.) . . . . . . . . . . . . . . . . . . . . . .37, 77
dinner party (n.) . . . . . . . . . . . . . . . . . . .77
dip (v.) . . . . . . . . . . . . . . . . . . . . . . . . . . .18
directions (n.) . . . . . . . . . . . . . . . . . . . . .27
dirt (n.) . . . . . . . . . . . . . . . . . . . . . . . . . .28
dirty (adj.) . . . . . . . . . . . . . . . . . . .36, 39, 46
disc (n.) . . . . . . . . . . . . . . . . . . . . . . . . . .40
     (see also *CD, compact disc*)
dish (n.) . . . . . . . . . . . . . . . . . .38, 39, 52, 53
     (see also *serving dish*)
dish soap (n.) . . . . . . . . . . . . . . . . . . . . . .39
do (v.) . . . . . . . . . . . . . . . . . . . . . . . . . . .45
do dishes (v.) . . . . . . . . . . . . . . . . . . . . . .39
do laundry (v.) . . . . . . . . . . . . . . . . . . . . .48
     (see also *laundry, laundry basket*)
dog (n.) . . . . . . . . . . . . . . . . . . . . . . . . . .53
done (adj.) . . . . . . . . . . . . . . .16, 35, 38, 41, 42
door (n.) . . . . . . . . . . . . . . . . . . .19, 20, 30, 31
down (adv.) . . . . . . . . . . . . . . . . . . . . . . . .23
     (see also *up and down*)
down (see *sit down, slow down, turn down*)
drain (n.) . . . . . . . . . . . . . . . . . . . . . . . . .39
drain (v.) . . . . . . . . . . . . . . . . . . . . . . .32, 35

draw (v.) . . . . . . . . . . . . . . . . . . . . . . . . .45
dress (n.) . . . . . . . . . . . . . . . . . . . . . . . . .12
dress (see *get dressed*)
dressing (n.) . . . . . . . . . . . . . . . . . . . . . . .32
drill (n.) . . . . . . . . . . . . . . . . . . . . . . . . . .61
drill (v.) . . . . . . . . . . . . . . . . . . . . . . . . . .61
drink (n.) . . . . . . . . . . . . . . . . . . . . . . . . .79
drink (v.) . . . . . . . . . . . . . . . . . . . . . . . . .18
drip (v.) . . . . . . . . . . . . . . . . . . . . . . . .15, 39
drive (v.) . . . . . . . . . . . . . . . . . . . . . . . . .24
driver (n.) . . . . . . . . . . . . . .20, 21, 22, 25, 27
driveway (n.) . . . . . . . . . . . . . . . . . . . . . .22
drop off (v.) . . . . . . . . . . . . . . . . . . . . . . .45
dry (v.) . . . . . . . . . . . . . . . . . . .9, 39, 49, 56
dry off (v.) . . . . . . . . . . . . . . . . . . . . . .7, 9
dryer (n.) . . . . . . . . . . . . . . . . . . . . . . . . .49
dust (v.) . . . . . . . . . . . . . . . . . . . . . . . . . .50
dustpan (n.) . . . . . . . . . . . . . . . . . . . . . . .51

## E

earphones (n.) . . . . . . . . . . . . . . . . . . . . .41
eat (v.) . . . . . . . . . . . . . .7, 18, 36, 37, 76, 79
egg (n.) . . . . . . . . . . . . . . . . . . . . . . . .17, 18
eject (v.) . . . . . . . . . . . . . . . . . . . .40, 41, 44
electric (adj.) . . . . . . . . . . . . . . . . . . . . . .15
elevator (n.) . . . . . . . . . . . . . . . . . . . . . . .30
empty (adj.) . . . . . . . . . . . . . . . . . . . . . . .21
empty (v.) . . . . . . . . . . . . . . . . . . . . . . . . .51
end (n.) . . . . . . . . . . . . . . . . . . . . . . . . . .44
endorse (v.) . . . . . . . . . . . . . . . . . . . . . . .66
enter (v.) . . . . . . . . . . . . . . . . . . . . . . .25, 67
envelope (n.) . . . . . . . . . . . . . . . . . . . .74, 75
erase (v.) . . . . . . . . . . . . . . . . . . . . . . . . .72
estimate (n.) . . . . . . . . . . . . . . . . . . . . . . .57
exit (v.) . . . . . . . . . . . . . . . . . . . . . . . . . .25
express (adj.) . . . . . . . . . . . . . . . . . . . . . .75
extra (adj.) . . . . . . . . . . . . . . . . . . . . . . . .55

## F

face (n.) . . . . . . . . . . . . . . . . . . . . . . . . . .46
failure (n.) . . . . . . . . . . . . . . . . . . . . . . . .59
fall asleep (v.) . . . . . . . . . . . . . . . . . . . . .47
fare (n.) . . . . . . . . . . . . . . . . . . . . . . . .21, 27
fast (adv.) . . . . . . . . . . . . . . . . . . . . . .23, 41
fasten (v.) . . . . . . . . . . . . . . . . . . . . . . . . .11
fastener (n.) . . . . . . . . . . . . . . . . . . . . . . .11
fast food (n.) . . . . . . . . . . . . . . . . . . . . . .79
     (see also *food*)
fast-forward (v.) . . . . . . . . . . . . . . . . . . . .41
     (see also *forward*)
fat (n.) . . . . . . . . . . . . . . . . . . . . . . . . . . .34
fertilizer (n.) . . . . . . . . . . . . . . . . . . . . . .55
fill out (v.) . . . . . . . . . . . . . . . . . . . . . . . .66
     (see also *out*)
filter (n.) . . . . . . . . . . . . . . . . . . . . . . . . .15
finally (adv.) . . . . . . . .40, 47, 55, 56, 58, 63
find (v.) . . . . . . . . . . . . . . . . . . . . . . . .42, 59
finish (v.) . . . . . . . . . . . . . . . . . . . . . . .18, 79
finished (adj.) . . . . . . . . . . . . . . . . . . . . . .79
fitted (adj.) . . . . . . . . . . . . . . . . . . . . . . . .14

fix (v.) . . . . . . . . . . . . . . . . . . . . . . . . . . .22
flashlight (n.) . . . . . . . . . . . . . . . . . . . . . .59
     (see also *light*)
flat (adj.) . . . . . . . . . . . . . . . . . . . . . . .14, 58
flip (v.) . . . . . . . . . . . . . . . . . . . . . . . . . . .17
floor (n.) . . . . . . . . . . . . . . . . . .30, 50, 51, 56
floss (n.) . . . . . . . . . . . . . . . . . . . . . . . . . .8
floss (v.) . . . . . . . . . . . . . . . . . . . . . . . . . .8
flower (n.) . . . . . . . . . . . . . . . . . . . . . . . .55
fluff up (v.) . . . . . . . . . . . . . . . . . . . . . . . .14
     (see also *up*)
flush (v.) . . . . . . . . . . . . . . . . . . . . . . . . . .6
fold (v.) . . . . . . . . . . . . . . . . . . . . . . . .49, 74
follow (v.) . . . . . . . . . . . . . . . . . . . . . . . .26
food (n.) . . . . . . . . . . . . . . . . .37, 50, 52, 53, 79
     (see also *fast food*)
foot (n.) . . . . . . . . . . . . . . . . . . . . . . . .14, 23
fork (n.) . . . . . . . . . . . . . . . . . . . . . . . .18, 37
forward (adv.) . . . . . . . . . . . . . . . . . . .40, 41
     (see also *fast-forward*)
freeway (n.) . . . . . . . . . . . . . . . . . . . . . . .25
friend (n.) . . . . . . . . . . . . . .22, 24, 73, 74, 76
frozen (adj.) . . . . . . . . . . . . . . . . . . . . . . .63
fruit (n.) . . . . . . . . . . . . . . . . . . . . . . . . . .62
fry (v.) . . . . . . . . . . . . . . . . . . . . . . . . .17, 34
frying pan (n.) . . . . . . . . . . . . . . . . . . . . .17
     (see also *pan*)
full (adj.) . . . . . . . . . . . . . . . . . . . . . . . . .21

## G

game show (n.) . . . . . . . . . . . . . . . . . . . . .43
garage (n.) . . . . . . . . . . . . . . . . . . . . . . . .57
garbage (n.) . . . . . . . . . . . . . . . . . . . . .38, 51
garden (n.) . . . . . . . . . . . . . . . . . . . . . . . .55
gardening (n.) . . . . . . . . . . . . . . . . . . . . . .55
gas (n.) . . . . . . . . . . . . . . . . . . . . . .23, 25, 54
gas station (n.) . . . . . . . . . . . . . . . . . . . . .25
     (see also *station*)
gate (n.) . . . . . . . . . . . . . . . . . . . . . . . . . .26
gear (n.) . . . . . . . . . . . . . . . . . . . . . . . .23, 29
gearshift (n.) . . . . . . . . . . . . . . . . . . . . . .23
get (v.) . . . . . . . .30, 36, 41, 56, 62, 63, 71, 79
get dressed (v.) . . . . . . . . . . . . . . . .7, 10, 12
get home (v.) . . . . . . . . . . . . . . . . . . . . . .72
     (see also *home*)
get in (v.) . . . . . . . . . . . . . . . . . . . . . . . . .27
get into (v.) . . . . . . . . . . . . . . . . . . . . . . .47
get off (v.) . . . . . . . . . . . . .21, 25, 26, 29, 30
get on (v.) . . . . . . . . . . . . . .20, 25, 26, 29, 30
get out (v.) . . . . . . . . . . . . . . . . . . . . . . . .24
get up (v.) . . . . . . . . . . . . . . . . . . . . . . . . .6
     (see also *up*)
give (v.) . . . .21, 24, 27, 57, 64, 65, 66, 67, 76,
     77, 79
give back (v.) . . . . . . . . . . . . . . . . . . . . . .66
glass (n.) . . . . . . . . . . . . . . . . . . . . . . . . .37
glasses (n.) . . . . . . . . . . . . . . . . . . . . . . . .10
glove (n.) . . . . . . . . . . . . . . . . . . . . . . . . .13
glue (n.) . . . . . . . . . . . . . . . . . . . . . . . . . .60
go (v.) . . 23, 24, 25, 27, 28, 29, 30, 31, 39, 40,
     41, 43, 46, 63, 66, 67, 75, 76, 78

go back (v.) . . . . . . . . . . . . . . . . . . . . .30, 31
go barefoot (v.) . . . . . . . . . . . . . . . . . . . .13
go into (v.) . . . . . . . . . . . . . . . . . . . . . . . .6
good-bye (see *say good-bye*)
go out (v.) . . . . . . . . . . . . . . . . . . . . . .7, 59
   (see also *out*)
go over (v.) . . . . . . . . . . . . . . . . . . . . . . .24
good night (see *say good night*)
go to (v.) . . . . . . . . . . . . . . . . . . . . . . . . .77
grass (n.) . . . . . . . . . . . . . . . . . . . . . . . . .54
grater (n.) . . . . . . . . . . . . . . . . . . . . . . . .32
green (adj.) . . . . . . . . . . . . . . . . . . . . . . .24
greet (v.) . . . . . . . . . . . . . . . . . . . . . . . . .77
greeting (n.) . . . . . . . . . . . . . . . . . . . . . .73
groceries (n.) . . . . . . . . . . . . . . . . . . . . .62
ground (adj.) . . . . . . . . . . . . . . . . . . . . . .15
ground beef (n.) . . . . . . . . . . . . . . . . . . .34
guest (n.) . . . . . . . . . . . . . . . . . . . . . . . . .77

### H

hail (v.) . . . . . . . . . . . . . . . . . . . . . . . . . .27
hair (n.) . . . . . . . . . . . . . . . . . . . . . . . . .7, 9
hall (n.) . . . . . . . . . . . . . . . . . . . . . . . . . .30
hammer (n.) . . . . . . . . . . . . . . . . . . . . . .60
hand (n.) . . . . . . . . . . . . . . . . . . . . . . . . . .6
   (see also *by hand, shake hands*)
handlebars (n.) . . . . . . . . . . . . . . . . . . . .29
hang (v.) . . . . . . . . . . . . . . . . . . . . . . . . .31
hang out (v.) . . . . . . . . . . . . . . . . . . . . . .49
   (see also *out*)
hang up (v.) . . . . . . . . . . . . . . . . . .46, 49, 69
   (see also *up*)
happy (adj.) . . . . . . . . . . . . . . . . . . . . .52, 76
hat (n.) . . . . . . . . . . . . . . . . . . . . . . . . . .13
have (has) (v.) . . . . . . . . . . . . . . . .18, 37, 58
have dinner (v.) . . . . . . . . . . . . . . . . . . . .77
head (n.) . . . . . . . . . . . . . . . . . . . . . . . . .14
hear (v.) . . . . . . . . . . . . . .26, 43, 68, 69, 72
heat (n.) . . . . . . . . . . . . . . . . . . . . . . .35, 36
heat (v.) . . . . . . . . . . . . . . . . . . .34, 36, 49
heat up (v.) . . . . . . . . . . . . . . . . . . . . . . .15
   (see also *up*)
heavy (adj.) . . . . . . . . . . . . . . . . . . . . . . .13
hello (see *say hello*)
helmet (n.) . . . . . . . . . . . . . . . . . . . . . . .29
hill (n.) . . . . . . . . . . . . . . . . . . . . . . . . . .29
hold (v.) . . . . . . . . . . . . . . . . . . . . . . .29, 61
hold on (v.) . . . . . . . . . . . . . . . . . . . . . . .21
hole (n.) . . . . . . . . . . . . . . . . . . . . . . . . . .61
home (adv.) . . . . . . . . . . . . . . . . . . . . . . .30
   (see also *get home*)
hose (n.) . . . . . . . . . . . . . . . . . . . . . . .54, 55
host (n.) . . . . . . . . . . . . . . . . . . . . . . . . . .77
hot (adj.) . . . . . . . . . . . . . . . . . . . . . . .13, 15
house (n.) . . . . . . . . . . . . . . . . . . .19, 31, 50
hubcap (n.) . . . . . . . . . . . . . . . . . . . . . . .58

### I

ice cream (n.) . . . . . . . . . . . . . . . . . . . . .76

ID (identification) (n.) . . . . . . . . . . . . . . .65
in line (adv'l.) . . . . . . . . . . . . . . . . . . .75, 79
index (n.) . . . . . . . . . . . . . . . . . . . . . . .42, 55
insect (n.) . . . . . . . . . . . . . . . . . . . . . . . . .55
insecticide (n.) . . . . . . . . . . . . . . . . . . . . .55
inside (adv.) . . . . . . . . . . . . . . . . . . . . .30, 77
inside (n.) . . . . . . . . . . . . . . . . . . . . . . . . .56
interesting (adj.) . . . . . . . . . . . . . . . . . . .42
intersection (n.) . . . . . . . . . . . . . . . . . . . .24
introduce (v.) . . . . . . . . . . . . . . . . . . . . . .77
iron (n.) . . . . . . . . . . . . . . . . . . . . . . . . . .49
iron (v.) . . . . . . . . . . . . . . . . . . . . . . . . . .49

### J

jack up (v.) . . . . . . . . . . . . . . . . . . . . . . . .58
   (see also *up*)
jacket (n.) . . . . . . . . . . . . . . . . . .10, 12, 19
jam (n.) . . . . . . . . . . . . . . . . . . . . . . . . . .16
jar (n.) . . . . . . . . . . . . . . . . . . . . . . . . . . .51
jeans (n.) . . . . . . . . . . . . . . . . . . . . . . . . .12
join (v.) . . . . . . . . . . . . . . . . . . . . . . .60, 61
jump (v.) . . . . . . . . . . . . . . . . . . . . . . . . .52

### K

key (n.) . . . . . . . . . . . . . . . . .19, 22, 64, 67
kitchen (n.) . . . . . . . . . . . . . . . . . . .38, 43, 50
knife (n.) . . . . . . . . . . . . . . . . . . .16, 18, 37
know (v.) . . . . . . . . . . . . . . . . . . . . . . . . .69

### L

lace (n.) . . . . . . . . . . . . . . . . . . . . . . . . . .11
lace up (v.) . . . . . . . . . . . . . . . . . . . . . . . .11
   (see also *up*)
lamp (n.) . . . . . . . . . . . . . . . . . . . . . . . . .47
lane (n.) . . . . . . . . . . . . . . . . . . . . . . . . . .25
lap (n.) . . . . . . . . . . . . . . . . . . . . . . . . . . .37
large (adj.) . . . . . . . . . . . . . . . . . . . . . . . .35
last name (n.) . . . . . . . . . . . . . . . . . . . . . .70
late (adj.) . . . . . . . . . . . . . . . . . . . . . . . . .28
late (adv.) . . . . . . . . . . . . . . . . . . . . . . . . .46
later (adv.) . . . . . . . . . .44, 45, 53, 57, 71, 77
laundry (n.) . . . . . . . . . . . . . . . . . . . . .48, 49
   (see also *do laundry*)
laundry basket (n.) . . . . . . . . . . . . . . .46, 48
lawn (n.) . . . . . . . . . . . . . . . . . . . . . . . . .54
leash (n.) . . . . . . . . . . . . . . . . . . . . . . . . .53
leave (v.) . . . . . . . . . .18, 19, 44, 70, 71, 78
leave (a message) (v.) . . . . . . . . . . . . . . .72
leaves (n.) . . . . . . . . . . . . . . . . . . . . . .15, 55
left (adv.) . . . . . . . . . . . . . . . . . . . . . . .25, 74
leftovers (n.) . . . . . . . . . . . . . . . . . . . . . .38
let up on (v.) . . . . . . . . . . . . . . . . . . . . . .23
letter (n.) . . . . . . . . . . . . . . . . . . .73, 74, 75
lettuce (n.) . . . . . . . . . . . . . . . . . . . . . . . .32
lever (n.) . . . . . . . . . . . . . . . . . . . . . . . . .16
lid (n.) . . . . . . . . . . . . . . . . . . . . . . . . .33, 36
lie down (v.) . . . . . . . . . . . . . . . . . . . . . . .47
light (adj.) . . . . . . . . . . . . . . . . . . . . . . .13, 48

light (n.) . . . . . . . . . . . . . . . . . .23, 24, 47
   (see also *flashlight*)
light (v.) . . . . . . . . . . . . . . . . . . . .17, 59, 76
like (v.) . . . . . . . . . . . . . . . . . . . . . . . . . . .43
line up (v.) . . . . . . . . . . . . . . . . . . . . . . . .67
   (see also *up*)
liquid (n.) . . . . . . . . . . . . . . . . . . . . . . . . .35
list (n.) . . . . . . . . . . . . . . . . . . . . . . . . . . .62
listen (v.) . . . . . . . . . . . . . . . . . . . . . . . . .69
listen to (v.) . . . . . . . . . . . . . . . . . . . . .40, 72
litter box (n.) . . . . . . . . . . . . . . . . . . . . . .52
living room (n.) . . . . . . . . . . . . . . . . . .31, 50
   (see also *room*)
lock (v.) . . . . . . . . . . . . . . . . . . . . . . .24, 29
   (see also *unlock*)
long-sleeved (adj.) . . . . . . . . . . . . . . . . . .13
   (see also *short-sleeved*)
look (v.) . . . . . . . . . . . . . . . . . . . . . . . . . .22
look at (v.) . . . . . . . . . . . . . . . . . . . . . .42, 73
look for (v.) . . . . . . . . . . . . . . . . . . . . . . . .63
look through (v.) . . . . . . . . . . . . . . . . . . . .42
look up (v.) . . . . . . . . . . . . . . . . . . . . .42, 68
   (see also *up*)
loosen (v.) . . . . . . . . . . . . . . . . . . . . . . . .61
loud (adj.) . . . . . . . . . . . . . . . . . . . . . . . .41
lower (adj.) . . . . . . . . . . . . . . . . . . . . . . . .29
lower (v.) . . . . . . . . . . . . . . . . . . . . . . . . .58
lunch (n.) . . . . . . . . . . . . . . . . . . . . . . . . .79

### M

machine (n.) . . . . . . . . . . .21, 26, 48, 49, 67
   (see also *answering machine*)
magazine (n.) . . . . . . . . . . . . . . . . . . . . . .42
mail (n.) . . . . . . . . . . . . . . . . . . . . . . .30, 31
mail (v.) . . . . . . . . . . . . . . . . . . . . . . . . . .74
mailbox (n.) . . . . . . . . . . . . . . . . . . . .30, 75
make (v.) . . . . . . .7, 15, 16, 32, 34, 40, 60, 68
make a bed (v.) . . . . . . . . . . . . . . . . . . . .14
man (n.) . . . . . . . . . . . . . . . . . . . . . . .10, 21
mark (v.) . . . . . . . . . . . . . . . . . . . . . . . . .60
mattress (n.) . . . . . . . . . . . . . . . . . . . . . . .14
measure (v.) . . . . . . . . . . . . . . . . . . . . . . .60
meat (n.) . . . . . . . . . . . . . . . . . . . . . . .34, 63
mechanic (n.) . . . . . . . . . . . . . . . . . . . . . .57
melt (v.) . . . . . . . . . . . . . . . . . . . . . . . . . .17
melted (adj.) . . . . . . . . . . . . . . . . . . . . . . .35
menu (n.) . . . . . . . . . . . . . . . . . . . . . . . . .79
message (n.) . . . . . . . . . . . . . . . . . .70, 71, 72
message light (n.) . . . . . . . . . . . . . . . . . . .72
meter (n.) . . . . . . . . . . . . . . . . . . . . . . . . .27
middle (n.) . . . . . . . . . . . . . . . . . . . . . . . .74
milk (n.) . . . . . . . . . . . . . . . . . . . . . . .16, 63
minute (n.) . . . . . . . . . . . . . . . . . . . . . . . .36
mirror (n.) . . . . . . . . . . . . . . . . . . . . . .22, 51
mitten (n.) . . . . . . . . . . . . . . . . . . . . . . . .13
mix (v.) . . . . . . . . . . . . . . . . . . . . . . . . . . .32
money (n.) . . . . . . . . . . . . . . . . . .21, 64, 67
mop (n.) . . . . . . . . . . . . . . . . . . . . . . . . . .51
mop (v.) . . . . . . . . . . . . . . . . . . . . . . . . . .51
more (adj.) . . . . . . . . . . . . . . . . . . . . . . . .37

mouth (n.) . . . . . . . . . . . . . . . . . . . . . . . .8, 18
move (v.) . . . . . . . . . . . . . . . . . . . . .8, 22, 29
movie (n.) . . . . . . . . . . . . . . . . . . . . . . . . . .78
mower (n.) . . . . . . . . . . . . . . . . . . . . . . . . . .54
music (n.) . . . . . . . . . . . . . . . . . . . . . . .40, 41
myself (pron.) . . . . . . . . . . . . . . . . . . . . . . .73

## N

nail (n.) . . . . . . . . . . . . . . . . . . . . . . . . . . . .60
name (n.) . . . . . . . . . . . . . . . . . . . . . . . . . . .70
napkin (n.) . . . . . . . . . . . . . . . . . . . .18, 37, 79
near (prep.) . . . . . . . . . . . . . . . . . . . . . . . . .21
need (v.) . . . . . . . . . . . . . . . . . . . . . . . .67, 75
neutral (n.) . . . . . . . . . . . . . . . . . . . . . . . . .23
new (adj.) . . . . . . . . . . . . . . . . . . . . . . . . . .42
news (n.) . . . . . . . . . . . . . . . . . . . . . . . . . . .43
newspaper (n.) . . . . . . . . . . . . . . . . . . . . . . .51
    (see also *paper*)
next (adj.) . . . . . . . . . . . . . . . . . . . . . . . . . .40
next to (prep.) . . . . . . . . . . . . . . . . . . . . . . .47
night (n.) . . . . . . . . . . . . . . . . . . . . . . . . . . .23
nightgown (n.) . . . . . . . . . . . . . . . . . . . . . . .46
notes (n.) . . . . . . . . . . . . . . . . . . . . . . . . . .72
number (n.) . . . . . . . . . . . . . . . . . . .40, 66, 68
    (see also *phone number, wrong number*)
nut (n.) . . . . . . . . . . . . . . . . . . . . . . . . .58, 61

## O

off (adv.) . . . . . . . . . . . . . . . . . . . . . . . . . . .59
offer (v.) . . . . . . . . . . . . . . . . . . . . . . . . . . .71
officer (n.) . . . . . . . . . . . . . . . . . . . . . . . . . .24
oil (n.) . . . . . . . . . . . . . . . . . . . . . . . . . . . . .25
old (adj.) . . . . . . . . . . . . . . . . . . . . . . . . . . .51
on (adv.) . . . . . . . . . . . . . . . . . . . . . . . . . . .43
on time (adv'l.) . . . . . . . . . . . . . . . . . . . . . .20
on top (adv'l.) . . . . . . . . . . . . . . . . . . . . . . .32
onion (n.) . . . . . . . . . . . . . . . . . . . . . . . .34, 35
open (v.) . . . . . . .19, 20, 30, 31, 41, 42, 52, 76
order (v.) . . . . . . . . . . . . . . . . . . . . . . . . . . .79
other (adj.) . . . . . . . . . . . . . . . . . .21, 26, 45, 77
    (see also *another*)
out (adv.) . . . . . . . . . . . . . . . . . . . . . . . .48, 49
    (see also *back out of, blow out, fill out, go
    out, hang out, pull out, smooth out, take
    out, take out of, throw out*)
outside (adv.) . . . . . . . . . . . . . . . . . . . . . . . .19
outside (n.) . . . . . . . . . . . . . . . . . . . . . . . . .56
over (adv.) . . . . . . . . . . . . . . . . . . . . . . . . . .43
over (prep.) . . . . . . . . . . . . . . . . . . . . . . .14, 28
overpass (n.) . . . . . . . . . . . . . . . . . . . . . . . .28

## P

page (n.) . . . . . . . . . . . . . . . . . . . . . . . . . . .42
pajamas (n.) . . . . . . . . . . . . . . . . . . . . . . . . .10
pan (n.) . . . . . . . . . . . . . . . . . . .17, 33, 34, 35
    (see also *frying pan*)
panties (n.) . . . . . . . . . . . . . . . . . . . . . . . . .12
pants (n.) . . . . . . . . . . . . . . . . . . .10, 11, 12, 13
pantyhose (n.) . . . . . . . . . . . . . . . . . . . . . . .12

paper (n.) . . . . . . . . . . . . . . . . . . . . . . . .18, 73
    (see also *newspaper, toilet paper*)
parent (n.) . . . . . . . . . . . . . . . . . . . . . . .45, 46
park (v.) . . . . . . . . . . . . . . . . . . . . . . . . . . . .24
parking lot (n.) . . . . . . . . . . . . . . . . . . . . . . .28
part (n.) . . . . . . . . . . . . . . . . . . . . . . . . . . . .42
party (n.) . . . . . . . . . . . . . . . . . . . . . . . . . . .76
pass (n.) . . . . . . . . . . . . . . . . . . . . . . . . . . . .21
pass (v.) . . . . . . . . . . . . . . . . . . . . . . . . .25, 37
passbook (n.) . . . . . . . . . . . . . . . . . . . . . . . .66
passenger (n.) . . . . . . . . . . . . . . . . . . . . . . . .26
pause (v.) . . . . . . . . . . . . . . . . . . . . . . . .41, 44
pay (v.) . . . . . . . . . .21, 25, 27, 64, 65, 79
payment slip (n.) . . . . . . . . . . . . . . . . . . . . . .65
pedal (n.) . . . . . . . . . . . . . . . . . . . . . . . .23, 29
pedal (v.) . . . . . . . . . . . . . . . . . . . . . . . . . . .29
peel (v.) . . . . . . . . . . . . . . . . . . . . . . . . .16, 33
people (n.) . . . . . . . . . . . . . . . . .12, 21, 77, 79
person (n.) . . . . . . . . . . . . . . . . . . . . . . . . . .69
personal (adj.) . . . . . . . . . . . . . . . . . . . . . . .73
pet (v.) . . . . . . . . . . . . . . . . . . . . . . . . . .52, 53
phone (n.) . . . . . . . . . . . . . . . . . . . .68, 69, 71
    (see also *telephone*)
phone message (n.) . . . . . . . . . . . . . . . . . . . .31
phone number (n.) . . . . . . . . . . . . . . . . . . . . .70
    (see also *number, wrong number*)
pick (v.) . . . . . . . . . . . . . . . . . . . . . . . . .40, 55
pick up (v.) . . . . 10, 19, 31, 40, 42, 43, 45, 50,
    68, 69
    (see also *up*)
picture (n.) . . . . . . . . . . . . . . . . . . . .42, 45, 74
piece (n.) . . . . . . . . . . . . . . . . . . . . . . . .35, 60
pillow (n.) . . . . . . . . . . . . . . . . . . . . . . . . . .14
PIN (n.) . . . . . . . . . . . . . . . . . . . . . . . . . . . .67
pizza (n.) . . . . . . . . . . . . . . . . . . . . . . . . . . .63
place (n.) . . . . . . . . . . . . . . . . . . . . . . . . . . .60
plane (n.) . . . . . . . . . . . . . . . . . . . . . . . . . . .60
plant (n.) . . . . . . . . . . . . . . . . . . . . . . . . . . .55
plant (v.) . . . . . . . . . . . . . . . . . . . . . . . . . . .55
plate (n.) . . . . . . . . . . . . . . . . . . .17, 35, 37, 38
play (v.) . . . . . . . . . . . . . . . . . . .40, 41, 45, 52
play (a message) (v.) . . . . . . . . . . . . . . . . . . .72
player (n.) . . . . . . . . . . . . . . . . . . . . . . . .40, 41
playground (n.) . . . . . . . . . . . . . . . . . . . . . . .45
pliers (n.) . . . . . . . . . . . . . . . . . . . . . . . . . . .61
plug (n.) . . . . . . . . . . . . . . . . . . . . . . . . . . . .39
plug in (v.) . . . . . . . . . . . . . . . . . . . . . . . . . .41
pocket (n.) . . . . . . . . . . . . . . . . . . . . . . . .19, 48
police (n.) . . . . . . . . . . . . . . . . . . . . . . . . . .24
pop up (v.) . . . . . . . . . . . . . . . . . . . . . . . . . .16
    (see also *up*)
popcorn (n.) . . . . . . . . . . . . . . . . . . . . . . . . .78
postage (n.) . . . . . . . . . . . . . . . . . . . . . . . . .75
post office (n.) . . . . . . . . . . . . . . . . . . . . . . .74
pot (n.) . . . . . . . . . . . . . . . . . . . . . . . . . . . .36
pound (n.) . . . . . . . . . . . . . . . . . . . . . . . . . .63
pour (v.) . . . . . . . . . . . . . . .15, 16, 32, 35, 36
pour off (v.) . . . . . . . . . . . . . . . . . . . . . . .34, 36
power (n.) . . . . . . . . . . . . . . . . . . . . . . . . . .59
prepare (v.) . . . . . . . . . . . . . . . . . . . . . . .16, 33
present (n.) . . . . . . . . . . . . . . . . . . . . . . . . . .76
press (v.) . . . . . . . . . . . . .21, 30, 64, 67, 72

press in (v.) . . . . . . . . . . . . . . . . . . . . . . . . .40
preview (n.) . . . . . . . . . . . . . . . . . . . . . . . . .78
price (n.) . . . . . . . . . . . . . . . . . . . . . . . . . . .63
print (v.) . . . . . . . . . . . . . . . . . . . . . . . . .65, 66
problem (n.) . . . . . . . . . . . . . . . . . . . . . . . . .57
puddle (n.) . . . . . . . . . . . . . . . . . . . . . . . . . .28
pull (v.) . . . . . . . . . . . . . . . . . . . . . . . . . .14, 39
pull back (v.) . . . . . . . . . . . . . . . . . . . . . . . . .47
pull out (v.) . . . . . . . . . . . . . . . . . . . . . . . . . .8
    (see also *out*)
pull over (v.) . . . . . . . . . . . . . . . . . . . . . . . . .25

pull up (v.) . . . . . . . . . . . . . . . . . . . . . . .11, 14
    (see also *up*)
pump (n.) . . . . . . . . . . . . . . . . . . . . . . . . . . .25
pump (v.) . . . . . . . . . . . . . . . . . . . . . . . . . . .25
purchase (n.) . . . . . . . . . . . . . . . . . . . . . . . .64
purr (v.) . . . . . . . . . . . . . . . . . . . . . . . . . . . .52
push (v.) . . . . . . . . . . . . . . . . . . . . . . . . . . .54
push down (v.) . . . . . . . . . . . . . . . . . . . . . . .16
put (v.) . . .8, 9, 14, 15, 21, 31, 32, 33, 35, 36,
    37, 38, 39, 40, 41, 44, 45, 46, 47, 48, 49, 51,
    52, 53, 54, 55, 56, 61, 62, 64, 67, 71, 74, 75
put away (v.) . . . . . . . . . . . . . . . . . . .8, 39, 49
put back (v.) . . . . . . . . . . . . . . . . . . . . . . . . .41
put in (v.) . . . . . . . . . . . . . . . . . . . . .19, 22, 48
put into (v.) . . . . . . . . . . . . . . . . . . . . . . .17, 26
put on (v.) . . . . 10, 11, 12, 13, 16, 17, 19, 23,
    29, 31, 41, 58
put out (v.) . . . . . . . . . . . . . . . . . . . . . . . . . .51
puzzle (n.) . . . . . . . . . . . . . . . . . . . . . . . . . .45

## Q

question (n.) . . . . . . . . . . . . . . . . . . . . . . . . .73

## R

rack (n.) . . . . . . . . . . . . . . . . . . . . . . . . .29, 39
rain (v.) . . . . . . . . . . . . . . . . . . . . . . . . . . . .23
rake (n.) . . . . . . . . . . . . . . . . . . . . . . . . . . . .54
rake (v.) . . . . . . . . . . . . . . . . . . . . . . . . . . . .54
read (v.) . . . . . . . . . . . . .18, 21, 42, 45, 47, 79
ready (adj.) . . . . . . . . . . . . . . . . . . . . . . . . . .36
receipt (n.) . . . . . . . . . . . . . . . . . . . . .21, 64, 65
record (v.) . . . . . . . . . . . . . . . . . . . . . . . .65, 72
recycling (n.) . . . . . . . . . . . . . . . . . . . . . . . .51
recycling box (n.) . . . . . . . . . . . . . . . . . . . . .51
red (adj.) . . . . . . . . . . . . . . . . . . . . . . . . . . .24
refrigerator (n.) . . . . . . . . . . . . . . . . . . . . .38, 50
register (n.) . . . . . . . . . . . . . . . . . . . . . . . . . .64
regular (adj.) . . . . . . . . . . . . . . . . . . . . . . . . .75
remote (n.) . . . . . . . . . . . . . . . . . . . . . . . .40, 43
rent (v.) . . . . . . . . . . . . . . . . . . . . . . . . . . . .44
repair (n.) . . . . . . . . . . . . . . . . . . . . . . . . . . .57
repeat (v.) . . . . . . . . . . . . . . . . . . . . . . . .40, 70
reset (v.) . . . . . . . . . . . . . . . . . . . . . . . . . . .59
restaurant (n.) . . . . . . . . . . . . . . . . . . . . . . . .79
return (v.) . . . . . . . . . . . . . . . . . . . . .30, 44, 67
rewind (v.) . . . . . . . . . . . . . . . . . . . . . . . .41, 44
rice (n.) . . . . . . . . . . . . . . . . . . . . . . . . . . . .36
ride (n.) . . . . . . . . . . . . . . . . . . . . . . . . . . . .21

ride (v.) . . . . . . . . . . . . . . . . . . . . . . . . . . .29
right (adv.) . . . . . . . . . . . . . . . . . . . . . . . . .25
right of way (n.) . . . . . . . . . . . . . . . . . . . . .25
ring (v.) . . . . . . . . . . . . . . . . . . . . . . . . .68, 69
ring up (v.) . . . . . . . . . . . . . . . . . . . . . . . . .64
   (see also *up*)
rinse (v.) . . . . . . . . . . . . . . . . . . . . .39, 49, 56
rinse off (v.) . . . . . . . . . . . . . . . . . . . . . . . .8, 9
road (n.) . . . . . . . . . . . . . . . . . . . . . . . . . . .25
room (n.) . . . . . . . . . . . . . . . . . . . . . . . . . . .48
   (see also *bathroom, living room*)
ruler (v.) . . . . . . . . . . . . . . . . . . . . . . . . . . .60
run (v.) . . . . . . . . . . . . . . . . . . . . . . . . . . . .28
run water over (v.) . . . . . . . . . . . . . . . . . . . .8
running shoe (n.) . . . . . . . . . . . . . . . . . . . .12
   (see also *shoe*)

## S

salad (n.) . . . . . . . . . . . . . . . . . . . . . . . .32, 37
salad bowl (n.) . . . . . . . . . . . . . . . . . . . . . .37
sand (v.) . . . . . . . . . . . . . . . . . . . . . . . . . . .60
sandal (n.) . . . . . . . . . . . . . . . . . . . . . .12, 13
sandpaper (n.) . . . . . . . . . . . . . . . . . . . . . .60
sauce (n.) . . . . . . . . . . . . . . . . . . . . . . . . . .35
   (see also *tomato sauce*)
saucer (n.) . . . . . . . . . . . . . . . . . . . . . . . . .37
saw (n.) . . . . . . . . . . . . . . . . . . . . . . . . . . .60
say (v.) . . . . . . . . . . . . . . . . . . . . . . . . . . . .70
say good-bye (v.) . . . . . . . . . . . . . . . . . . . .19
say good night (v.) . . . . . . . . . . . . . . . .46, 77
say hello (v.) . . . . . . . . . . . . . . . . . .68, 69, 77
scan (v.) . . . . . . . . . . . . . . . . . . . . . . . . . . .64
scarf (n.) . . . . . . . . . . . . . . . . . . . . . . . . . . .13
schedule (n.) . . . . . . . . . . . . . . . . . . . . . . .20
scrape (v.) . . . . . . . . . . . . . . . . . . . . . . . . . .38
screw (n.) . . . . . . . . . . . . . . . . . . . . . . .60, 61
screwdriver (n.) . . . . . . . . . . . . . . . . . .60, 61
scrub (v.) . . . . . . . . . . . . . . . . . . . . . . . .39, 51
seal (v.) . . . . . . . . . . . . . . . . . . . . . . . . . . . .74
seat (n.) . . . . . . . . . . . . . . . . . . . . . .21, 22, 78
seat belt (n.) . . . . . . . . . . . . . . . . . . . . . . . .22
see (v.) . . . . . . . . . . . . . . . . . . . .42, 44, 72, 78
seed (n.) . . . . . . . . . . . . . . . . . . . . . . . .54, 55
seedling (n.) . . . . . . . . . . . . . . . . . . . . . . . .55
serving dish (n.) . . . . . . . . . . . . . . . . . . . . .38
set (v.) . . . . . . . . . . . . . . . . . . . . . . . . . .47, 48
set (a table) (v.) . . . . . . . . . . . . . . . . . . . . . .37
setting (n.) . . . . . . . . . . . . . . . . . . . . . . . . .44
shake hands (v.) . . . . . . . . . . . . . . . . . . . . .77
shampoo (n.) . . . . . . . . . . . . . . . . . . . . . . . .9
shave (v.) . . . . . . . . . . . . . . . . . . . . . . . . . . .7
sheet (n.) . . . . . . . . . . . . . . . . . . . . . . . . . . .14
shell (n.) . . . . . . . . . . . . . . . . . . . . . . . . . . .17
shift (v.) . . . . . . . . . . . . . . . . . . . . . . . . .23, 29
shift lever (n.) . . . . . . . . . . . . . . . . . . . . . . .29
shine (v.) . . . . . . . . . . . . . . . . . . . . . . . . . . .56
shirt (n.) . . . . . . . . . . . . . . . . . . . .10, 11, 12, 13
   (see also *T-shirt*)
shoe (n.) . . . . . . . . . . . . . . . . . . .10, 12, 19, 31
   (see also *running shoe*)
shop (v.) . . . . . . . . . . . . . . . . . . . . . . . . . . .62

shopper (n.) . . . . . . . . . . . . . . . . . . . . . . . .62
shopping (adj.) . . . . . . . . . . . . . . . . . . . . . .62
short (adj.) . . . . . . . . . . . . . . . . . . . . . . . . . .41
shorts (n.) . . . . . . . . . . . . . . . . . . . . .10, 12, 13
short-sleeved (adj.) . . . . . . . . . . . . . . . . . . .13
   (see also *long-sleeved*)
show (v.) . . . . . . . . . . . . . . . . . . . . . . . . . . .21
shower (n.) . . . . . . . . . . . . . . . . . . . . . . . .7, 9
shut (v.) . . . . . . . . . . . . . . . . . . . . . . . . . . . .19
side (n.) . . . . . . . . . . . . . . . . . . . . . . . . . . . .25
sidewalk (n.) . . . . . . . . . . . . . . . . . . . . . . . .28
sign (n.) . . . . . . . . . . . . . . . . . . . . . . . .24, 26
sign (v.) . . . . . . . . . . . . . . . . . . . . . . .65, 73, 76
signal (n.) . . . . . . . . . . . . . . . . . . . . . . . . . .23
sing (v.) . . . . . . . . . . . . . . . . . . . . . . . . . . . .76
sink (n.) . . . . . . . . . . . . . . . . . . . . . . .8, 39, 51
sister (n.) . . . . . . . . . . . . . . . . . . . . . . . . . . .59
sit (v.) . . . . . . . . . . . . . . . . . . . . . . . . . . . . .22
sit down (v.) . . . . . . . . . . . . . . .18, 20, 21, 37
skip (v.) . . . . . . . . . . . . . . . . . . . . . . . . . . . .40
skirt (n.) . . . . . . . . . . . . . . . . . . . . . . . . . . . .12
slice (n.) . . . . . . . . . . . . . . . . . . . . . . . . . . . .16
slice (v.) . . . . . . . . . . . . . . . . . . . . . .16, 32, 33
slip (v.) . . . . . . . . . . . . . . . . . . . . . . . . . .8, 14
slip on (v.) . . . . . . . . . . . . . . . . . . . . . . . . . .11
slot (n.) . . . . . . . . . . . . . . . . . . . . . . . . . . . .26
slow down (v.) . . . . . . . . . . . . . . . . . . . .23, 29
smell (v.) . . . . . . . . . . . . . . . . . . . . . . . . . . .62
smooth (adj.) . . . . . . . . . . . . . . . . . . . . . . . .60
smooth out (v.) . . . . . . . . . . . . . . . . . . . . . .14
   (see also *out*)
snap (n.) . . . . . . . . . . . . . . . . . . . . . . . . . . .11
snap (v.) . . . . . . . . . . . . . . . . . . . . . . . . . . .11
soap (n.) . . . . . . . . . . . . . . . . . . . . . . . . . . . .9
soapy (adj.) . . . . . . . . . . . . . . . . . . . . . . . . .56
sock (n.) . . . . . . . . . . . . . . . . . . . . . .10, 12, 13
soft (adj.) . . . . . . . . . . . . . . . . . . . . . . . . . . .41
soil (n.) . . . . . . . . . . . . . . . . . . . . . . . . . . . .55
solid (n.) . . . . . . . . . . . . . . . . . . . . . . . . . . .35
some (adj.) . .10, 18, 32, 33, 35, 37, 42, 46, 48,
  49, 52, 53, 54, 55, 56, 58, 59, 61, 62, 63, 64,
  72, 73, 74, 77, 78, 79
sometimes (adv.) . . . . . . . . . . .18, 21, 23, 28
somewhere (adv.) . . . . . . . . . . . . . . . . . . . .28
sort (v.) . . . . . . . . . . . . . . . . . . . . . . . . . . . .48
spaghetti (n.) . . . . . . . . . . . . . . . . . . . .34, 35
spare (adj.) . . . . . . . . . . . . . . . . . . . . . . . . .58
speak (v.) . . . . . . . . . . . . . . . . . . . . . . . . . . .70
special (n.) . . . . . . . . . . . . . . . . . . . . . . . . .63
speeding (n.) . . . . . . . . . . . . . . . . . . . . . . . .24
speed limit (n.) . . . . . . . . . . . . . . . . . . . . . .24
speed up (v.) . . . . . . . . . . . . . . . . . . . . . . . .23
   (see also *up*)
spell (v.) . . . . . . . . . . . . . . . . . . . . . . . . . . . .70
spice (n.) . . . . . . . . . . . . . . . . . . . . . . . . . . .35
spin (v.) . . . . . . . . . . . . . . . . . . . . . . . . . . . .49
spit (v.) . . . . . . . . . . . . . . . . . . . . . . . . . . . . .8
sponge (n.) . . . . . . . . . . . . . . . . . . . . . . . . .56
spoon (n.) . . . . . . . . . . . . . . . . . . . . . . .18, 37
spray (v.) . . . . . . . . . . . . . . . . . . . . . . . . . . .55
sprinkle (v.) . . . . . . . . . . . . . . . . . . . . . . . . .32
squeeze (v.) . . . . . . . . . . . . . . . . . . . . . . . . .29

stack (v.) . . . . . . . . . . . . . . . . . . . . . . . . . . .38
stake (n.) . . . . . . . . . . . . . . . . . . . . . . . . . . .55
stamp (n.) . . . . . . . . . . . . . . . . . . . . . . . . . .75
stand (v.) . . . . . . . . . . . . . . . . . . . . . . . .21, 26
start (v.) . . . . . .22, 27, 35, 36, 41, 44, 54, 73
station (n.) . . . . . . . . . . . . . . . . . . . . . . . . .26
   (see also *gas station*)
steam (n.) . . . . . . . . . . . . . . . . . . . . . . . . . .33
steam (v.) . . . . . . . . . . . . . . . . . . . . . . . . . .33
steamer basket (n.) . . . . . . . . . . . . . . . . . . .33
steering wheel (n.) . . . . . . . . . . . . . . . . . . .23
step (n.) . . . . . . . . . . . . . . . . . . . . . . . . . . . .31
step (v.) . . . . . . . . . . . . . . . . .9, 19, 23, 28
stick (n.) . . . . . . . . . . . . . . . . . . . . . . . . . . .53
stick on (v.) . . . . . . . . . . . . . . . . . . . . . . . . .75
stir (v.) . . . . . . . . . . . . . . . . . . . . . . .15, 34, 35
stocking (n.) . . . . . . . . . . . . . . . . . . . . . . . .12
stop (n.) . . . . . . . . . . . . . . . . . . . . . . . . .20, 21
stop (v.) . . . . .21, 23, 24, 25, 27, 28, 40, 41, 44
storm (n.) . . . . . . . . . . . . . . . . . . . . . . . . . .59
stove (n.) . . . . . . . . . . . . . . . . . . . . . . . . . . .17
straight (adv.) . . . . . . . . . . . . . . . . . . . . . . .25
straighten (v.) . . . . . . . . . . . . . . . . . . . . . . .11
strain (v.) . . . . . . . . . . . . . . . . . . . . . . . . . . .15
strainer (n.) . . . . . . . . . . . . . . . . . . . . . . . . .15
strap (n.) . . . . . . . . . . . . . . . . . . . . . . . . . . .21
straw (n.) . . . . . . . . . . . . . . . . . . . . . . . . . . .79
street (n.) . . . . . . . . . . . . . . . . . . . . . . . . . . .28
string (n.) . . . . . . . . . . . . . . . . . . . . . . . . . .52
strip (n.) . . . . . . . . . . . . . . . . . . . . . . . . . . . .67
sugar (n.) . . . . . . . . . . . . . . . . . . . . .15, 16, 35
suit (n.) . . . . . . . . . . . . . . . . . . . . . . . . . . . .12
sweater (n.) . . . . . . . . . . . . . . . . . . . . . . . . .13
sweatshirt (n.) . . . . . . . . . . . . . . . . . . . . . . .12
sweep (v.) . . . . . . . . . . . . . . . . . . . . . . .50, 51
swipe (v.) . . . . . . . . . . . . . . . . . . . . . . . . . .65
swish (v.) . . . . . . . . . . . . . . . . . . . . . . . . . . .8
switch (v.) . . . . . . . . . . . . . . . . . . . . . . . . . .44

## T

table (n.) . . . . . . . . . . . . . . . . . . . . .18, 37, 38
table of contents (n.) . . . . . . . . . . . . . . . . .42
tail (n.) . . . . . . . . . . . . . . . . . . . . . . . . . . . . .53
take (v.) . .8, 37, 38, 45, 48, 49, 53, 57, 63, 71,
  74, 79
take (a bath) (v.) . . . . . . . . . . . . . . . . . . . . .45
take (an elevator) (v.) . . . . . . . . . . . . . . . . .30
take (a shower) (v.) . . . . . . . . . . . . . . . . . .7, 9
take (a taxi) (v.) . . . . . . . . . . . . . . . . . . . . . .27
take (a train) (v.) . . . . . . . . . . . . . . . . . . . . .26
take care of (v.) . . . . . . . . .45, 52, 53, 54, 55
take (notes) (v.) . . . . . . . . . . . . . . . . . . . . . .72
take off (v.) . . . . . . . . . . . . . . . . . . .23, 31, 58
take out (v.) . . . .17, 40, 41, 44, 58, 64, 67, 73
   (see also *out*)
take out of (v.) . . . . . . . . . . . . . . . . . . . .48, 49
talk (v.) . . . . . . . . . . . . . . . .18, 37, 68, 69, 77
tape (n.) . . . . . . . . . . . . . . . . . . . . . . . . .41, 44
taxi (n.) . . . . . . . . . . . . . . . . . . . . . . . . . . . .27
tea (n.) . . . . . . . . . . . . . . . . . . . . . . . . . .15, 18
teacup (n.) . . . . . . . . . . . . . . . . . . . . . . . . . .15

teapot (n.) . . . . . . . . . . . . . . . . . . . . . .15
tear (v.) . . . . . . . . . . . . . . . . . . . . . . . .78
telephone (n.) . . . . . . . . . . . . . . . . . . . .69
   (see also *phone*)
television (n.) . . . . . . . . . . . . . . . . . . . .43
   (see also *TV*)
tell (v.) . . . . . . . . . . .25, 27, 57, 64, 69, 73
teller (n.) . . . . . . . . . . . . . . . . . . . . . . .66
thank (v.) . . . . . . . . . . . . . . . . . . . . . . .77
there (adv.) . . . . . . . . . . . . . . . . . . . . . .71
thing (n.) . . . . . . . . . . . . .48, 49, 50, 61, 64
through (prep.) . . . . . . . . . . . . . . . . .28, 61
throw (v.) . . . . . . . . . . . . . . . . . . . . . . .53
throw out (v.) . . . . . . . . . . . . . . . .17, 50, 79
   (see also *out*)
ticket (n.) . . . . . . . . . . . . . . . . . .24, 26, 78
ticket-taker (n.) . . . . . . . . . . . . . . . . . . .78
tie (n.) . . . . . . . . . . . . . . . . . . . . . . . . .12
tie (v.) . . . . . . . . . . . . . . . . . . . . . .11, 55
tie up (v.) . . . . . . . . . . . . . . . . . . . . . . .51
tighten (v.) . . . . . . . . . . . . . . . . . . . .58, 61
time (n.) . . . . . . . . . . . . . . . . . . . . . . . .41
tip (n.) . . . . . . . . . . . . . . . . . . . . . . . . .27
tire (n.) . . . . . . . . . . . . . . . . . . . . . . . . .58
title (n.) . . . . . . . . . . . . . . . . . . . . . . . .42
toast (n.) . . . . . . . . . . . . . . . . . . . . .16, 18
toast (v.) . . . . . . . . . . . . . . . . . . . . . . . .16
toaster (n.) . . . . . . . . . . . . . . . . . . . . . .16
toilet (n.) . . . . . . . . . . . . . . . . . . .6, 46, 51
toilet paper (n.) . . . . . . . . . . . . . . . . . . .63
   (see also *paper*)
tomato (n.) . . . . . . . . . . . . . . . . . . . . . .32
tomato sauce (n.) . . . . . . . . . . . . . . . . . .34
   (see also *sauce*)
tooth (teeth) (n.) . . . . . . . . . . . . . . .7, 8, 46
toothbrush (n.) . . . . . . . . . . . . . . . . . . . .8
toothpaste (n.) . . . . . . . . . . . . . . . . . . . .8
top (adj.) . . . . . . . . . . . . . . . . . . . . . . . .14
top (n.) . . . . . . . . . . . . . . . . . . . . . . . . .61
total (adj.) . . . . . . . . . . . . . . . . . . . . . . .66
total (n.) . . . . . . . . . . . . . . . . . . . . .64, 66
towel (n.) . . . . . . . . . . . . . . . . . . . .7, 9, 39
track (n.) . . . . . . . . . . . . . . . . . . . . . . . .40
traffic light (n.) . . . . . . . . . . . . . . . . . . .24
train (n.) . . . . . . . . . . . . . . . . . . . . . . . .26
trash (n.) . . . . . . . . . . . . . . . . . . . . . . . .79
tray (n.) . . . . . . . . . . . . . . . . . . . . . . . . .40
tree (n.) . . . . . . . . . . . . . . . . . . . . . . . . .54
trim (v.) . . . . . . . . . . . . . . . . . . . . . .54, 60
trip (v.) . . . . . . . . . . . . . . . . . . . . . . . . .28

trunk (n.) . . . . . . . . . . . . . . . . . . . . . . . .58
T-shirt (n.) . . . . . . . . . . . . . . . . . . . . .10, 12
   (see also *shirt*)
tuck (v.) . . . . . . . . . . . . . . . . . . . . . . . .14
tuck in (v.) . . . . . . . . . . . . . . . . . . . . . . .11
turn (n.) . . . . . . . . . . . . . . . . . . . . . . . .75
turn (v.) . . . . . . . . . .22, 23, 25, 34, 42, 55, 61
turn down (v.) . . . . . . . . . . . . . . . .35, 36, 41
   (see also *down*)
turn off (v.) . . . . . . . . . . .9, 24, 34, 43, 47
turn on (v.) 9, 15, 17, 23, 33, 43, 44, 47, 48, 59
turn up (v.) . . . . . . . . . . . . . . . . . . .41, 43
   (see also *up*)
TV (n.) . . . . . . . . . . . . . . . . . . . . . .43, 45
   (see also *television*)

## U

uncle (n.) . . . . . . . . . . . . . . . . . . . . . . .45
under (prep.) . . . . . . . . . . . . . . . . . . . . .14
underpants (n.) . . . . . . . . . . . . . . . . . . .10
underwear (n.) . . . . . . . . . . . . . . . . . . . .10
unlock (v.) . . . . . . . . . . . . . . . . . . . . . . .31
   (see also *lock*)
up (adv.) . . . . . . . . . . . . . . . . . . . . .23, 29
   (see also *fluff up, get up, hang up, heat up, jack up, lace up, line up, look up, pick up, pop up, pull up, ring up, speed up, turn up, up and down, wake up, zip up*)
up and down (adv'l.) . . . . . . . . . . . . . . . .8
   (see also *down, up*)
upper (adj.) . . . . . . . . . . . . . . . . . . . . . .74
upstairs (adv.) . . . . . . . . . . . . . . . . . . . .46
use (v.) . . . . . . . . .6, 40, 41, 43, 46, 62, 67, 72

## V

vacuum (v.) . . . . . . . . . . . . . . . . . . .50, 56
vacuum cleaner (n.) . . . . . . . . . . . . . . . .50
VCR (n.) . . . . . . . . . . . . . . . . . . . . . . . .44
vegetable (n.) . . . . . . . . . . . . . . . . . .33, 62
video (n.) . . . . . . . . . . . . . . . . . . . . . . .44
volume (n.) . . . . . . . . . . . . . . . . . . . . . .43

## W

wag (v.) . . . . . . . . . . . . . . . . . . . . . . . . .53
wait (v.) . . . . . .15, 20, 26, 28, 30, 36, 75, 79
wake up (v.) . . . . . . . . . . . . . . . . . . . . . .6
   (see also *up*)

walk (n.) . . . . . . . . . . . . . . . . . . . . . . . .53
walk (v.) . . . . . . . . . . . .20, 26, 28, 30, 31
wallet (n.) . . . . . . . . . . . . . . . . . . . . . . .19
want (v.) . . . . . . . . . . . . . . . . . .25, 40, 44
wash (v.) . . . . . .6, 9, 32, 33, 39, 46, 49, 51, 56
washer (n.) . . . . . . . . . . . . . . . . . . . . . .61
washing machine (n.) . . . . . . . . . . . . . . .48
wastebasket (n.) . . . . . . . . . . . . . . . . . . .51
watch (v.) . . . . . . . . . . . . . . . .43, 44, 45, 78
water (n.) . . .8, 9, 15, 33, 35, 36, 39, 52, 53, 56
water (v.) . . . . . . . . . . . . . . . . . . . . .54, 55
wax (n.) . . . . . . . . . . . . . . . . . . . . . . . . .56
wear (v.) . . . . . . . . . . . . . . . . . . . . .12, 13
weather (n.) . . . . . . . . . . . . . . . . . . . . . .13
weed (v.) . . . . . . . . . . . . . . . . . . . . . . . .55
weigh (v.) . . . . . . . . . . . . . . . . . . . .62, 75
wet (adj.) . . . . . . . . . . . . . . . . . . . . . . . .49
where (adv.) . . . . . . . . . . . . . . . . . . . . . .27
white (n.) . . . . . . . . . . . . . . . . . . . . . . . .17
window (n.) . . . . . . . . . . . . . . . . .26, 56, 75
wine (n.) . . . . . . . . . . . . . . . . . . . . . . . .77
wipe (v.) . . . . . . . . . . . . . . . . . . . . .18, 50
wipe off (v.) . . . . . . . . . . . . . . . . . . .38, 56
wiper (n.) . . . . . . . . . . . . . . . . . . . . . . .23
woman (n.) . . . . . . . . . . . . . . . . . . . . . .12
wood (n.) . . . . . . . . . . . . . . . . . . . . . . . .60
word (n.) . . . . . . . . . . . . . . . . . . . . . . . .42
work (adj.) . . . . . . . . . . . . . . . . . . . . . . .31
work (v.) . . . . . . . . . . . . . . . . . . . . . . . .60
work on (v.) . . . . . . . . . . . . . . . . . . . . . .57
wrap (v.) . . . . . . . . . . . . . . . . . . . . . .9, 76
wrench (n.) . . . . . . . . . . . . . . . . . . .58, 61
write (v.) . . . . . . . . . . . .65, 66, 71, 73, 74
wrong number (n.) . . . . . . . . . . . . . . . . .69
   (see also *number, phone number*)

## Y

yawn (v.) . . . . . . . . . . . . . . . . . . . . . . . .46
yield (v.) . . . . . . . . . . . . . . . . . . . . . . . .25
yolk (n.) . . . . . . . . . . . . . . . . . . . . . . . . .17

## Z

zip up (v.) . . . . . . . . . . . . . . . . . . . .11, 19
   (see also *up*)
zipper (n.) . . . . . . . . . . . . . . . . . . . . . . .11

# IRREGULAR FORMS

## Verbs

| Be | Have |
|---|---|

I am . . . . . . . . . . . . . . . . . . .I have

You are . . . . . . . . . . . . . .You have

He is . . . . . . . . . . . . . . . . .He has

She is . . . . . . . . . . . . . . . .She has

We are . . . . . . . . . . . . . .We have

They are . . . . . . . . . . . .They have

## Noun Plurals

| Singular (One) | Plural (More than One) |
|---|---|

child . . . . . . . . . . . . . . . . .children

foot . . . . . . . . . . . . . . . . . . . . .feet

knife . . . . . . . . . . . . . . . . . .knives

leaf . . . . . . . . . . . . . . . . . . . .leaves

man . . . . . . . . . . . . . . . . . . . . .men

person . . . . . . . . . . . . . . . .people

tooth . . . . . . . . . . . . . . . . . . .teeth

woman . . . . . . . . . . . . . . .women

# Process:

## Key Vocabulary

- - - - - - - - - - - - - - - - - -
- - - - - - - - - - - - - - - - - -
- - - - - - - - - - - - - - - - - -
- - - - - - - - - - - - - - - - - -
- - - - - - - - - - - - - - - - - -
- - - - - - - - - - - - - - - - - -
- - - - - - - - - - - - - - - - - -
- - - - - - - - - - - - - - - - - -
- - - - - - - - - - - - - - - - - -
- - - - - - - - - - - - - - - - - -
- - - - - - - - - - - - - - - - - -
- - - - - - - - - - - - - - - - - -
- - - - - - - - - - - - - - - - - -
- - - - - - - - - - - - - - - - - -
- - - - - - - - - - - - - - - - - -
- - - - - - - - - - - - - - - - - -
- - - - - - - - - - - - - - - - - -
- - - - - - - - - - - - - - - - - -
- - - - - - - - - - - - - - - - - -
- - - - - - - - - - - - - - - - - -
- - - - - - - - - - - - - - - - - -

# Process:

## Key Vocabulary

# Process:

## Key Vocabulary

- - - - - - - - - - - - - - - - - - - - - -
- - - - - - - - - - - - - - - - - - - - - -
- - - - - - - - - - - - - - - - - - - - - -
- - - - - - - - - - - - - - - - - - - - - -
- - - - - - - - - - - - - - - - - - - - - -
- - - - - - - - - - - - - - - - - - - - - -
- - - - - - - - - - - - - - - - - - - - - -
- - - - - - - - - - - - - - - - - - - - - -
- - - - - - - - - - - - - - - - - - - - - -
- - - - - - - - - - - - - - - - - - - - - -
- - - - - - - - - - - - - - - - - - - - - -
- - - - - - - - - - - - - - - - - - - - - -
- - - - - - - - - - - - - - - - - - - - - -
- - - - - - - - - - - - - - - - - - - - - -
- - - - - - - - - - - - - - - - - - - - - -
- - - - - - - - - - - - - - - - - - - - - -
- - - - - - - - - - - - - - - - - - - - - -
- - - - - - - - - - - - - - - - - - - - - -
- - - - - - - - - - - - - - - - - - - - - -
- - - - - - - - - - - - - - - - - - - - - -
- - - - - - - - - - - - - - - - - - - - - -

# Process:

## Key Vocabulary

- - - - - - - - - - - - - - - -
- - - - - - - - - - - - - - - -
- - - - - - - - - - - - - - - -
- - - - - - - - - - - - - - - -
- - - - - - - - - - - - - - - -
- - - - - - - - - - - - - - - -
- - - - - - - - - - - - - - - -
- - - - - - - - - - - - - - - -
- - - - - - - - - - - - - - - -
- - - - - - - - - - - - - - - -
- - - - - - - - - - - - - - - -
- - - - - - - - - - - - - - - -
- - - - - - - - - - - - - - - -
- - - - - - - - - - - - - - - -
- - - - - - - - - - - - - - - -
- - - - - - - - - - - - - - - -
- - - - - - - - - - - - - - - -
- - - - - - - - - - - - - - - -
- - - - - - - - - - - - - - - -
- - - - - - - - - - - - - - - -
- - - - - - - - - - - - - - - -
- - - - - - - - - - - - - - - -

# Process:

## Key Vocabulary

- - - - - - - - - - - - - - - - - - -
- - - - - - - - - - - - - - - - - - -
- - - - - - - - - - - - - - - - - - -
- - - - - - - - - - - - - - - - - - -
- - - - - - - - - - - - - - - - - - -
- - - - - - - - - - - - - - - - - - -
- - - - - - - - - - - - - - - - - - -
- - - - - - - - - - - - - - - - - - -
- - - - - - - - - - - - - - - - - - -
- - - - - - - - - - - - - - - - - - -
- - - - - - - - - - - - - - - - - - -
- - - - - - - - - - - - - - - - - - -
- - - - - - - - - - - - - - - - - - -
- - - - - - - - - - - - - - - - - - -
- - - - - - - - - - - - - - - - - - -
- - - - - - - - - - - - - - - - - - -
- - - - - - - - - - - - - - - - - - -
- - - - - - - - - - - - - - - - - - -
- - - - - - - - - - - - - - - - - - -
- - - - - - - - - - - - - - - - - - -

# Process:

## Key Vocabulary

- - - - - - - - - - - - - - - -
- - - - - - - - - - - - - - - -
- - - - - - - - - - - - - - - -
- - - - - - - - - - - - - - - -
- - - - - - - - - - - - - - - -
- - - - - - - - - - - - - - - -
- - - - - - - - - - - - - - - -
- - - - - - - - - - - - - - - -
- - - - - - - - - - - - - - - -
- - - - - - - - - - - - - - - -
- - - - - - - - - - - - - - - -
- - - - - - - - - - - - - - - -
- - - - - - - - - - - - - - - -
- - - - - - - - - - - - - - - -
- - - - - - - - - - - - - - - -
- - - - - - - - - - - - - - - -
- - - - - - - - - - - - - - - -
- - - - - - - - - - - - - - - -
- - - - - - - - - - - - - - - -
- - - - - - - - - - - - - - - -
- - - - - - - - - - - - - - - -
- - - - - - - - - - - - - - - -
- - - - - - - - - - - - - - - -

# Notes to the Teacher

Basic *English for Everyday Activities* helps students learn vocabulary for daily processes by associating the vocabulary with pictures. The text is accessible to low-beginning learners, but even high-beginning and intermediate learners, uncertain about the English of everyday life, will find Basic *English for Everyday Activities* useful. Higher-level students will appreciate finally finding out the word for putting shirttails into pants (tuck) or using water to get the soap off something (rinse).

A recording of this text is available (separately) to help students learn the spoken forms of this vocabulary. The recording features native speakers of North American English and includes both the captions and the dialogue that accompany the pictures. A workbook for reading, writing, and discussion is also available to make a multi-skill course in everyday vocabulary.

## Aims

A few of the aims central to Basic *English for Everyday Activities* are:

- To activate the reader's event schemata—expectations about how ordinary activities usually proceed.
- To concentrate on the most essential and picturable steps in those activities.
- To focus on verbs, since they are the key to communicating about everyday events.
- To present nouns and other words as they are used with verbs to talk about activities.
- To create pictorial associations for key vocabulary.

## Organization

Each chapter focuses narrowly on one process and depicts it in one or two pages. Some sub-processes are grouped within a large one, as indicated by an extra heading at the top of the page. For example, "Making Coffee / Making Tea," "Preparing Cold Cereal / Making Toast," and "Frying an Egg" are all part of a "Making Breakfast" sequence.

The chapters are grouped into six larger sections. Each section could form a unit in a course syllabus. However, the chapters of Basic *English for Everyday Activities* are independent of one another and do not have to be used sequentially. If your students have no interest in learning the language for, say, driving a car, they can easily skip Chapters 13–15 without being hampered in their work with later chapters.

At the back of the book, you will find several important elements:

- Common Measurements, Days, Months, and Numbers will help students from outside the United States convert the measurements mentioned in the text into units familiar to them.
- Charts of Fahrenheit and Celsius temperatures and U.S. money denominations give students this information to include in their speaking and writing.
- A list of days of the week, months of the year, and numbers will aid students as they talk about dates, times, and money amounts.
- The index is an invaluable tool for looking up familiar vocabulary and for broadening a sense of the contexts in which a word may be used.
- Following the index, Irregular Forms includes two basic verbs, *to be* and *to have*, and some irregular plural noun forms.
- On the templates, Processes: My Way, students can write their own versions of daily processes—either variations on those in the book or other processes that do not appear here. These template pages may be photocopied.

## Working with Low-Beginning Students

In working with beginners, you will find it useful to introduce and practice the lesson vocabulary orally, both nouns and verbs, before students use the textbook. The processes can be performed or acted out as students practice responding to command forms of the process steps. Students can give each other commands as they perform the steps. After students are familiar with the vocabulary, they can point out the objects and activities in the pictures before listening to and reading the corresponding captions in the lesson.

## Individualizing the Material

The templates (pages 90–95) acknowledge a basic fact about everyday processes: each student has his or her own schemata for them. Each person's experience, expectations, and habits vary somehow from any "basic" way of describing the process. A student is unlikely to start her day or make his bed exactly as pictured in the book. But the basic sequences given here can be valuable springboards for class or group discussions and for writing about individual differences. Working with the template or with other tools for encouraging individual expression, students can put their new vocabulary to work in describing their own ways of doing things.